"If you have a film or TV concept you want to pitch . . . *and sell* . . . then Heather's book is your secret weapon. Every page has nuggets of impossible-to-find info to make your concept stand out."

 —JEANNE SIMON, content creator/TV pitch expert

"There are plenty of books about screenwriting and filmmaking, but none on how to actually sell projects. Hale fills that void with a comprehensive guide to developing, marketing and pitching that demystifies the process."

 —ERIK BORK, Emmy-winning writer-producer of HBO's *Band of Brothers*

"It's hard as hell to tell a great story. Everything after is harder still. Writers—take a minute to bitch and whine about it, then buck up and buy Heather's book about getting your masterpiece off your screen and onto everyone else's. It's your GPS for how to get to here from there."

 —JEFF ARCH, Academy Award–nominee, *Sleepless in Seattle*

"What a wealth of information! It can bring you . . . well, wealth! I only wish *StorySelling* had been around when I was starting out. It's BRILLIANT!"

 —SUZANNE LYONS, producer, Snowfall Films, Producers Guild of America member

"If you want to learn how to summarize your stories succinctly and express them entertainingly— on the page and in the room— then *StorySelling* is a must-have, imperative for your career."

 —BOB KOSBERG, The Pitch King, MoviePitch.com

"Heather has done a huge favor for all writers: she knows and shows how to market your story to get it made and told in today's world and the future. Consummate and helpful start to finish."

 —DAVE WATSON, *Walkabout Undone*; editor, Movies Matter

"Your story will never see the light of day unless someone buys the project. This book gives you the tools and resources to make sure your project gets what it deserves—a buyer.'"

 —RIC VIERS, producer, author

D1601713

"Insightful. Concise. Bursting with current market data. Hard-to-find resources clearly explained. This is by far the best book out there on this subject."

—ANNE MARIE GILLEN, producer, *Under Suspicion, Fried Green Tomatoes*; author, *The Producer's Business Handbook*

"Very complete. Extremely useful and well written. Encouraging. Accessible. All writers who want to sell their work need to have this in their libraries. Read it, study it, apply it!"

—DR. LINDA SEGER, author of *Making a Good Script Great*

"All of Heather's experience, insights, techniques and coaching brilliance have been gathered into this one book. Now it's in your hands. You're about to embark on a new journey that will not only put you in charge of your career, but will enhance your skills as a storyteller."

—MARK W. TRAVIS, director, writer, producer, coach

"So full of insider tips and the do's-and-don'ts of writing and *selling* scripts. An essential resource guide to the commercial elements of monetizing your words. Keep this book beside your writing space."

—ELLIOT GROVE, Raindance Film Festival

"Dang! What a great book! An easy-to-follow guide for everyone at whatever stage, age or page of your career."

—DEVO CUTLER-RUBENSTEIN, filmmaker/educator, former studio exec, Columbia Pictures TV

"A must-read primer before you get in there and pitch. Getting 'in the door' without this knowledge would destroy any potential chance you have for a deal. On the flip side, read this book and you've got the advantage on 99% of the people trying to sell."

—TOM MALLOY, producer/actor, author of *Bankroll*

"Heather Hale kills it in pitch meetings, on the page, and in this book. Read her and learn from the best."

—LAURA BRENNAN, writer/pitch consultant

STORY
SELLING

HOW TO DEVELOP, MARKET AND PITCH
FILM & TV PROJECTS

HEATHER HALE

MICHAEL WIESE PRODUCTIONS

Published by Michael Wiese Productions
12400 Ventura Blvd. #1111
Studio City, CA 91604
(818) 379-8799, (818) 986-3408 (FAX)
mw@mwp.com
www.mwp.com

Cover design by Johnny Ink. www.johnnyink.com
Interior design by William Morosi
Copyediting by David Wright
Printed by McNaughton & Gunn

Manufactured in the United States of America

Library of Congress Cataloging-in-Publication Data

Names: Hale, Heather, author.
Title: Storyselling : how to develop, market and pitch film & TV projects /
  by Heather Hale.
Description: Studio City, CA : Michael Wiese Productions, [2019]
Identifiers: LCCN 2018057724 | ISBN 9781615932818
Subjects: LCSH: Motion pictures--Marketing. | Television programs--Marketing.
Classification: LCC PN1995.9.M29 H353 2019 | DDC 384/.80688--dc23
LC record available at https://lccn.loc.gov/2018057724

CONTENTS

ADVANCED MARKETING & DEVELOPMENT DELIVERABLES

PITCHING 139

ACKNOWLEDGMENTS

First and foremost: Thank you, Ken Lee, for your benevolent patience.

I am grateful to finally be part of the Michael Wiese Productions' family of authors, all of whom have sung your allegiant praise for years, so many of whom I consider my friends and mentors. I am especially grateful to the kind professional guidance and genuine friendship over the years from Pamela Jaye Smith, Michael Hauge, Kathie Fong Yoneda, Linda Segar, Jen Grisanti and Mark Travis.

I am honored to join the MWP team, supporting conscious, positively charged media that emphasizes hope and affirms our shared values of trust, cooperation, self-empowerment, freedom, and love. I hope my book serves as a platform to further extend these noble efforts to encourage artists generating and disseminating the kind of content that not only heals those who encounter the art, but those who create it as well.

To all my MasterMinders, who are such keen sounding boards, tough decision vetters and, most importantly, whimsical joy-of-life virtuosos, most especially: Jenean Atwood Baynes, Andy Sobkovich, Xaque Gruber, Anne Marie Gillen, Suzanne Lyons, Gina Gladwell, Steve Barr, Erik Bork, Mark Harden and Steve Marston. And while not (yet) in one of my annual, organized peer groups, Jo Clark, Steve Kayser, and Cal Johnson, you three have absolutely been honorary MasterMinders to me. The LA Yahoo Producers Group and LA Confabbers have been great consistent resources.

Thanks to Master Cat José Silerio, Blake Snyder's former development exec, for sharing the ten *Save the Cat!* genre logline templates; Alex Elias, CEO, Qloo Inc., for allowing us to share the TasteDive.com image; IMDbPro and Variety Insight for allowing us permission to print screen grabs.

Special thanks to my Hail Mary pass receivers, who honored the call of a fellow writer, desperate for on-deadline feedback: James Moorer, Pat Mikulec, Jo Hannah Afton, David M. Jack, Rob Foster, Rennie Sharp, and A.J. Flick. *Thank You!*

Great gratitude to a few precious UCLA screenwriting teachers whose legacies still reverberate with me years later, whatever I write: Frank McAdams, Billy Mernit, and Tom Szollosi. The same holds true of Jeff Arch (*Sleepless in Seattle*), Terry Rossio (*Pirates of the Caribbean, Shrek*), Shane Black (*Lethal Weapon*), Jonathan Lynn (*My Cousin Vinny*), Zak Penn (*X-Men*) and Simon Kinberg (*Mr. and Mrs. Smith*), all of whom have been incredibly generous and kind advocates, educating and inspiring writers everywhere.

And sadly: Rest in Peace, Marrissa O'Leary and Jeff Wood. Both of you life-changing role models.

And, of course, Billy. Always Billy, who's everywhere, for everything. Thank you.

PREFACE

If you're reading this preface, it's reasonable to assume that you're a Story*Teller* who'd like to become a Story*Seller*. This book will help you achieve that goal.

You read the title, so you know what this book's about. A quick perusal of the table of contents will detail the full spectra of marketing materials and pitching scenarios covered. My hope is to acclimatize you to their cohesiveness so you can apply new mastery to your entire existing library and all your future projects.

Two decades supporting creatives striving to become artrepreneurs have revealed that the principles of pitching are universal and evergreen. Regardless of *What* you're pitching, *Where*, *When* and to *Whom*, it's the *How* — the approach strategies and assets engaged — that vary widely.

The research for this book was earned not only writing, developing, pitching, producing, and directing film and television projects, but also consulting, teaching, workshopping and coaching veterans and aspirants alike how to pitch, develop, write and edit content and complementary marketing materials. I've also produced dozens of pitch fests, writers' workshops and film and TV market events including customizing pitching workshops for ABC drama execs and master's degree students as well as conducting numerous "How to Pitch" interviews for the National Association of Television Program Executives (NATPE) and while writing my first book, *How to Work the Film & TV Markets: A Guide for Content Creators* (Focal Press).

STORYTELLERS CAN CHANGE THE WORLD.

We connect, we learn, we edify — and *we sell* — through story-telling. If you collaborate to use art to contextualize the human experience with the parallel goal of remuneration, then you're an *artrepreneur*.

And you have to pitch.

And pitch.

And pitch.

And write and rewrite.

And rewriteandrewriteandrewriteandrewrite!

It is my great hope that this book will help you in some small measure along your journey, empower you to capitalize on all the skills and resources already at your disposal and develop new insights and methodologies to become a success-ful — or even more successful — Story*Seller*.

INTRODUCTION

S tories inspire us. They help make sense of the world around us. They help us empathize with other worldviews and strive to understand life itself. Great cultural change has always been driven by creative innovators who manage to engage the public's imagination, ideally to make the world a better place. There is no higher calling.

But stories can't do any of that 'til they get out of the originator's head, onto the page and onto the world stage. It's not art 'til someone other than its creator encounters it.

Yet our modern global media and entertainment marketplace can feel overwhelming to content creators looking for practical points of access. Contemporary audiences are incredibly savvy — and inundated. They intersect with characters and storytelling worlds across multiple platforms, sometimes even simultaneously integrated.

Today, digital-native children are weaned on storytelling technology that used to be the exclusive domain of Hollywood studios. Many of the economic and knowledge barriers to entry have been annihilated, thus adding to the morass competing for the attention of the general public. Getting noticed — whether it's for a motion picture, television program, streaming content, published book, video game, or live event — can seem onerous if not impossible. And that's if you can even get through the series of quagmires to get *there*.

Before you even have the luxury of approaching *that* huge hurdle, you must first tackle all the other ultra-marathon milestones. Like getting someone — *anyone* — to read your script, watch your film, take a glance at your TV format — or heck, even just answer the phone or reply to a simple email query.

Feature screenwriters must first get someone to option or buy their speculative screenplay — or at least read it as evidence of skill to secure an assignment. Television scribes must entice an entity to develop, package, and set up their pilot. Independent film producers must convince not only equity financiers to invest in their movie to get it made, but then a distributor and/or international sales agent to sell the rights to exhibitors in territories around the world. Independent online content creators might turn to ad agencies and brands to help fund their programming.

All of these scenarios — and infinite variations — involve complex business-to-business sales. And that means getting the right information to the right people, at the right time, in the right ways. There is a huge difference between a screenwriter pitching herself to an agent or manager for representation versus an independent producer pitching a project to a prospective star or director attachment, compared to a reality TV host with a concept seeking to engage a coproduction partner versus how a studio or network advertises film and TV to the mass audience.

But that could actually be the trajectory of the exact same original idea, morphing through its ancillary markets and transmutations. The prospective customers at each node are as wildly different as are their starting point positionings, value propositions, and calls to action. But the guiding principles are the same. And while every type of project, person and sales scenario is undoubtedly unique, the real strategic value lies in the thinking: the advance planning and targeted preparation.

You learn to fish by fishing. By trial and error, you figure out the best hooks and bait to use for which fish. Proximity helps you network with veteran anglers who might humor you with some tricks to cleverly reel in different kinds of fish. Through camaraderie, they might even reveal a few secret fishing spots. Refining their experiences and practices, you evolve your own style, materials and techniques.

The Develop ∞ Market ∞ Pitch Continuum

Pitching is the engine of the development-marketing discovery process. These three phases inevitably overlap and incessantly interchange. Like lifting the leg of a three-legged stool, insights in one area raise the bar and require structural improvements to the other two. Pitch stumbles might reveal glaring problems inherent in the script. Pitchees' confused questions may highlight plot holes, credibility or pacing issues, demanding yet another rewrite. Clarifying character bios for your TV show bible might force you to rethink your entire series arc. Refining your pitch deck might cause you to hone your logline and revise your target audience and hit list. Like being stuck in *Groundhog Day*, "Development Hell" can feel like an infinite rewriting or editing loop, incessantly folding back in on itself. Scripts and films are never "perfect" — deadlines just coerce their release.

In an ideal world (that most can't locate), you pitch your script, it gets easily and quickly bought for seven figures and is seamlessly and joyfully produced into a financial and critical success by professionals that become like family. *Yay*, you!

But that's not how it normally pans out. Check your expectations. It's not uncommon to pitch — then get pitched *back*, by people who were not at all what they represented themselves to be. Or even if they are legit, they still might pitch back — the changes they would need you to make in order for them to actually proceed with your project. If you're lucky, you successfully turn *their version* into one you can all be satisfied with that (hopefully) they are in a position to fund, produce, and distribute.

Sometimes, instead of investing the time and energy speculatively writing an original spec script, a well-established screenwriter might pitch an idea in hopes of getting an entity to commission her writing that script. Or a producer might hire a writer to draft a treatment of what was well received in the room.

SPEC

A "spec" screenplay or treatment is written "speculatively" or "specced," meaning it was written in the writer's "free" time, on their own dime, with nobody "commissioning" (i.e., ordering or assigning) it, in hopes of identifying and submitting it to a prospect who might option or buy it in order to develop, finance, produce and/or distribute and market it.

It's a bit like building a house on spec, where you front the time, effort, expertise and expense with the intention of flipping it, finding someone who likes its architecture, colors and curb appeal enough to buy it just the way you built it.

The difference with a script or treatment is that it's but a literary blueprint, seeking someone else to front the money and take the risk to actually construct the house you described with words. That's a huge leap of faith — and one of the many reasons why selling the plan for a movie or television show is so hard. And why so much changes when dozens of other imaginations and areas of expertise begin barn-raising. The more specific your script, the more likely everyone will be making the same movie or TV show.

That is, if you can get them all on board in the first place.

The development process can zigzag in an endless maze, reminiscent of an impossible Escheresque staircase. You may invest years of your life in a single project — including exhausting the best of your creative energies and professional (and personal) relationships. Make sure the promise of each premise is worth the dedication it will require to see it to fruition.

Mise en Place → Mise en Scène

"Mise en place" is a culinary term that refers to the advance preparation and ordered arrangement of all a recipe's ingredients. This completely prepares a chef to pull everything together when the heat is on. This process emboldens her instincts to change proportions or even ingredients on the fly.

Feng shui relies on this philosophy as well, mandating "a place for everything and everything in its place." Even a chaotic kindergarten room can be organized in a flash provided there are color-coded drawers and cubbies with sufficient, obvious spaces for everything.

In pre-production, a director pulls together all the visual elements necessary to tell the story. She then decides what will be framed in the shot. This "mise en scène" encompasses everything from the actors' performances, wardrobe, hair, makeup and props to locations, sets and lighting.

Development is like that. You polish every component you might need and line them up, at the ready for any possible use or combination, rearranging them for each opportunity. As the process unfolds, you adjust the pitch. Like a director, you prepare and hope for magic. Whether you're a writer, producer or director — a chef, kindergarten teacher or parent — unpredictable obstacles can derail the best of intentions into disaster or create moments of delightful surprise that will become lifetime memories. . . and great stories!

Pitching film and television projects are complex sales, with long sales cycles, that usually have multiple decision-makers and stakeholders. During this research and development period, you prepare everything you might need, lining everything up in order: Mise en place.

Think of it as pre-production. Deciding which elements — in what proportions and combinations — should be in each marketing deliverable or verbal pitch for each prospect. Everything anyone would need to make a decision — and not a single thing more that could cause them to second-guess their interest.

Consider mise en scène as principal photography. It's when you're live and all your hard work in preparation must come together in an instant. It's your *Got Talent* audition, your Olympic event, your oner. Months to years to lives of hard work culminate in a performance under pressure. If it's excellent, lives are changed forever in seconds. Just like a pitch.

PRIMARY MARKETING DEVELOPMENT

Every industry, every product or service has a research and development phase. A learning process that helps define what it is you've got, what's working, what's not.

The best way to assess where your proposed project might best fit in the media marketplace is to study comps — comparable films or television programs — that predate yours and are relevant for one reason or another. Similar shows illustrate the landscape and illuminate your prospects. They help you fine-tune your own project by delineating what your project is like, what it's not like — and why.

What are the blockbuster benchmarks in your genre? What were the ratings favorites in your format? What cult classics define your genre? Does your project build upon them? What are the current critics' darlings? You must also study the bombs to differentiate how your project promises to avoid those pitfalls.

Comps = Your Project's Provenance

Think of comps as the "provenance" of your project. Provenance is documentation that tracks the lineage of a work of art, an antique or an archaeological discovery. It reveals where (and when) it came from and how it's changed hands over time, paper-trailing its origin to assure its chain of custody. A provenance evidences authenticity.

Critics, especially Internet Haters, often accuse Hollywood Greenlighters of being myopic when it comes to original material, only able to wrap their capitalistic minds around familiar, pre-sold, already "proven" franchises or remakes, with the consequent derivative diminishing returns, both creatively and financially. While this criticism might be valid in some cases, it is actually quite shortsighted when taken in light of the multi-screen, new media landscape we all find ourselves repurposing in.

Even for fresh, original ideas, comps provide some measure of comparing totally subjective art. There are all types of "comps." For ease and speed of read, we will start with creative and marketing comps and focus on financial comps under Business Plans.

Creative Comps

Usually the most fun and useful to writers, creative influences vary wildly by format and may include other intellectual property touchpoints such as iconic characters, graphic novels, Broadway musicals, children's storybooks and video games. Milestones of your genre or format may be used as sensibility references for style, tone, theme and issues raised.

Comp lists are uniquely specific. One comp might have an archetypical protagonist or antagonist; another might capture the mood; another, the milieu; while they all might reflect a certain Zeitgeist.

Creative comps offer greater freedom of breadth and depth than financial or marketing comps. You have the luxury to ignore financial or demographic relevance, even recency. It's alright if the budgets (of your creative comps) are way off from your realistic projection. Creative comps may be decades old or appeal to wildly different target audiences. Study previous models to ascertain how to contemporize or broaden yours. It's even okay to crisscross film and television (or other) formats. What matters is keen creative resonance to your specific project.

Today's content creators have the luxury of easy binge-watching on demand, unlike the primitive, pre-internet era, where we had to wait for a film to play at a local cineplex or tape reruns off TV onto VHS tape. But all your "competitors" have the same easy access to this bounty. Become versed in the classics as well as the little-known gems of your genre. They may have originally been blockbuster hits or labors of love with little fanfare that gained recognition via word-of-mouth over time, but "classics" are still relevant and enjoyed today.

COMP EXAMPLES

Classic Romantic Comedies

10 Things I Hate About You

27 Dresses

Bridget Jones's Diary

Chocolat

Clueless

Eternal Sunshine of the
Spotless Mind

Four Weddings and a Funeral

Groundhog Day

Hitch

How to Lose a Guy in 10 Days

Love Actually

Moonstruck

My Best Friend's Wedding

My Big Fat Greek Wedding

Notting Hill

Pretty Woman

Romancing the Stone

Sleepless in Seattle

Splash

The Princess Bride

Up in the Air

When Harry Met Sally

While You Were Sleeping

You've Got Mail

Festival Darlings & Indie Breakout Hits

500 Days of Summer

Amélie

Before Sunrise

Before Sunset

Being John Malkovich

Brokeback Mountain

Election

Juno

Little Miss Sunshine

Lost in Translation

Memento

Moonrise Kingdom

No Country for Old Men

Raising Arizona

Reservoir Dogs

Run Lola Run

Rushmore

Secretary

Sex, Lies and Videotape

Strictly Ballroom

The Usual Suspects

Thirteen

But. . . What Do You Actually Do
with Creative Comps?

Studying your project's precursors empowers it to stand on its antecedents' shoulders while clearly distinguishing your unique work from the canon. Creative comps help you identify structural elements, diagnose weaknesses, capitalize on strengths and maximize any missed opportunities. They can provide a curated catalog of on-point images to repurpose for your look books and rip-o-matics. And, as you'll read in "Prospecting," they also seed your Hit List.

Pursue the bread-crumb trails of success but investigate the footprints of failure, too. Don't ignore the massive flops; you'll have to disassociate yours soon enough. Although an indispensable resource to figure out what went wrong (and how you can do better), keep these creative comps a secret. Reserve these for internal development and discussion only with partners already officially attached to the project. Never reference them in any pitch or marketing materials. The mere whiff of failure can make most suits run.

This prep is priceless. If anyone ever throws one of these bombs in your face, you won't be blindsided. You'll be preloaded to confidently articulate how yours is different (read: superior) and won't suffer the same fate. Your specific market awareness may eclipse their fears and enhance their esteem for you. The backside of fear is hope — and that is what you're selling. Your confidence, clarity and passion fill sails.

Studying TV Creative Comps

If you're comparing your project to television series, study whatever scripts and episodes you can track down to study. Usually, you can at least secure the pilot script to read. Episodes are usually easy to find to view. You might even unearth comparable concepts that never made it to the screen or those cancelled after just the pilot or midway through Season One or Two. *Can you figure out why they failed?*

Watch at least the pilot of each creative comp to study each series' launching elements. Follow along on the script with a stopwatch in hand to track the show's pacing. View with focused intent. Take notes. Maintain a notebook or folders.

Popular, long-running shows promise an abundance of material. For key comps especially (if you have the time), you might watch the whole show from pilot to finale. If this is unrealistic, selectively study key episodes from each season; season premieres and finales, especially. But also look for episodes that won or were nominated for Emmys. These likely represent what their respective showrunners were most proud of, perceiving them as their strongest contenders.

Go to IMDb.com and click on the shows' "Awards" and see which specific episodes were nominated and watch as many of those as you can. These episodes are especially important.

Whether they won the awards or not is irrelevant. The showrunners (and/or the show's producers and/or distributors) submitted what *they thought* were their best episodes, so if you're pitching to them, these are the shows to be familiar with as they highlight what they thought was their best work. Also, looking at all the competing nominees in that specific category over the past few years might help you augment your list and enhance your knowledge.

Sweeps-week entries might be the least indicative of a given show as they often represent stunt-casted-cameo ratings grabs.

If it's a scripted show, your comp homework might illuminate the number of characters or story arcs that might work best for that type of show. If it's a game show or reality competition, study the mechanics of the show. *How are the contestants selected? Eliminated? Do the stakes escalate in each round?* If it's a lifestyle or build show: *What are the ins and outs? What's the throughline?* If it's a talk show: *Does the host segue to a field correspondent? Or transition to re-enactment footage? Does each episode begin and end on the same set? Does the host or the show engage with a studio or home audience? What's the set? Living room? Kitchen? Studio?* Simple building blocks.

If a show "jumped the shark"[1] (passed its peak of popularity), try to analyze some of the reasons the show went downhill — or how, when and why it picked up steam again. This can be priceless information to inform your own project development but also helps embolden your pitching confidence. Comps can be a powerful research-and-development tool to help you dramatically clarify and refine your project and prepare to pitch to those who make that kind of content.

Reach out to everyone you know in the industry to see if you can get your hands on the shows' bibles or formats[2] to study what got the shows sold in the first place or how their original vision might have evolved.

A great exercise is to reverse-engineer the show's bible yourself. What *might* they have contained? This is an incredibly fertile exercise to do for your very best comps — especially if they qualify across the board as creative, marketing and financial. . . even more so if you're pitching to their creators or distributors!

---

[1] Google it + "Fonzie" if need be.
[2] More on all these in their sections. If you need help sourcing material for educational research, e-mail me at *Author@HeatherHale.com* and I'll check my library or try to help you track down (but Google first, please).

Marketing Comps

It's prudent to study marketing comps for several reasons. They can serve as excellent case studies for everything from their loglines, taglines and key art[3] to help diagnose target audiences, brainstorm cast wish lists, study social media and advertising campaigns to distribution strategies. They may reveal geographical trends, the territories that might be most responsive to your project for presales (or to reserve for most profitability) or even ideas for festival premiere strategies.

If you can identify key cities with outsized affinity markets or relevant events, you might modify your predecessors' strategies. Boutique domestic distributors might be responsive to considering proposals enriched with suggested marketing campaigns or cascading distribution models. Fully funded independent producers can just hire service vendors to execute their plans. Marketing comps are also very relevant to TV producers raising funds for time buys and selling ad spots or internet content creators facilitating brand integration.

Writers typically focus on creative comps. But for many, a frustration with insufficient script sales and sluggish career traction can drive the most dedicated to shift into marketing their work like a producer, to ultimately producing their own projects. If your work as a writer is so good you don't need to wear any other hats, you're in rarefied air. However, most writers find themselves somewhere along that spectrum. Analyzing the key art and marketing campaigns of a project's comps can force everyone on the team to rethink how to best visually communicate a high-concept idea, crystallize murkier concepts and further elevate the script.

---

[3] I cover *key art* extensively in my first book, *How to Work the Film & TV Markets: A Guide for Content Creators*, but a sizeable excerpt, with full-color examples and a great creative brief, is available for free on my website at: *http://heatherhale.com/key-art*

HIGH CONCEPT

High concept is an ingenious idea that appeals to a mass audience. It can be communicated in just a few words, maybe a sentence, and its potential is obvious to all who hear it. It's the kind of idea that hits writers and producers with *"Why didn't I think of that?"* All genres and formats benefit from marketable high concepts. *Its importance cannot be overly emphasized.* While high concepts notoriously don't guarantee the resultant project will be good (or even profitable), they do help to secure pitch meetings, get scripts read and find audiences to pay to watch — all critical achievements.

HIGH-CONCEPT TV SHOW EXAMPLES

Awake (2012) After a car accident takes the life of a family member, a police detective lives two alternating parallel lives, one where his wife survived, the other, his son. *Is one of his "realities" merely a dream?*

Continuum (2012–2015) A detective from the year 2077 finds herself trapped in present-day Vancouver, searching for ruthless criminals from the future.

Designated Survivor (2016–2019) A low-level Cabinet member becomes President of the United States after a catastrophic attack kills everyone above him in the line of succession.

FlashForward (2009–2010) A special task force in the FBI investigates after every person on Earth simultaneously blacks out and awakens with a short vision of their future.

Frequency (2000) An accidental cross-time radio link connects father and son across 30 years. The son tries to save his father's life, but then must fix the consequences.

Jane the Virgin (2014 –) A young, devout Catholic woman discovers that she was accidentally artificially inseminated.

The Last Man on Earth (2015–2018) Almost two years after a virus wiped out most of the human race, Phil Miller only wishes for some company, but soon gets more than he bargained for when that company shows up in the form of other survivors.

The Last Ship (2014 –) The crew of a naval destroyer is forced to confront the reality of a new existence when a pandemic kills off most of Earth's population.

Limitless (2015–2016) An average twenty-eight-year-old man who gains the ability to use the full extent of his brain's capabilities is hired by the FBI as a consultant.

My Name Is Earl (2005–2009) A ne'er-do-well wins $100,000 in the lottery and decides to right all the wrongs from his past with his newfound realization.

Quantum Leap (1989–1993) Scientist Sam Beckett finds himself trapped in the past, "leaping" into the bodies of different people on a regular basis.

Wilfred (2011–2014) The story of a depressed man who inexplicably is the only one who can see his neighbor's dog as a full-grown man in a dog suit.

The Infamous Cross

Many pitchers will lead off or end a query or verbal pitch by crossing two movie or TV comps to illustrate what theirs "is like." *"It's X meets Y with a little bit of Z thrown in."* Of course, there can be mixed results with this. Your "pitchees" may have their own mixed feelings or preconceptions about those references. They may be thinking you mean something entirely different from what you're referencing, not be familiar with the program or, worse, be confused.

But these crosses work enough of the time that many people use them as a framing device. If it's really clear and you want to work this comparison into your pitch conversation, be as specific as possible about your meaning. Something like: *"It's got the bittersweet nostalgia of a Nicholas Sparks novel but with the irreverent comedy of Deadpool,*" so there's no question which specific elements you're likening yours to. Ideally, the two (or three) comps you're using qualify across the board as financial, marketing and creative comps — so they'll make sense on every front. If you have lots of comps this would work with, your project is probably too derivative. The cross should be a collision of ideas where the intersection teases your high concept. But if you have several to pick between, try to mix it up with a current hit, a blockbuster in the genre and something really unique to your project's sensibilities. Considering your comps in this way is invaluable, even if you never use this phrase. It helps you to further articulate your intentions (with or without the cross).

PEOPLE WHO LIKED THIS ALSO LIKED...

You're probably familiar with the Internet Movie Database (IMDb.com) and may even pay for their professional IMDb-Pro subscription. They have a consumer feature that currently is only available on the free version. So if you pay for the pro upgrade, you'll actually have to sign out to use this tool.

Under Videos and Photos, there is a header that reads "More Like This" under which they provide six or twelve algorithm-matched comps. You can flip through the titles, posters, loglines, ratings, genres, directors and stars and IMDb public ratings to see if any jump out at you as good comps to add to your research list.

The consumer version of IMDb.com (not Pro) suggests possible comparable programming.

You can dig one degree further by checking the respective comp lists of each of the original titles. This is a super handy speed reference but *beware*! It is absolutely an Internet Rabbit Hole (read: writers' time-suck procrastination device).

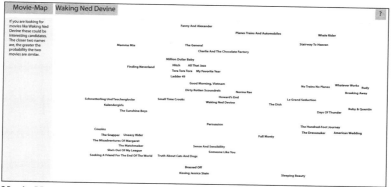

Movie-Map.com is another great resource to research comps.

TasteDive.com is yet another resource to research comps.

As IMDb is a public forum, a lot like Wikipedia, anything you post is visible to everyone. If you upgrade to Pro, you can add all your comps (or cast wish list) to a list titled after your project and share this with select colleagues.

2014	2010
Budget = $3.3M W.W.B.O. = $14M D: Sony Pictures Classics ISA: Sierra/Affinity Widest Release: 567 23 Weeks in Theaters Logline 3 Oscars | 74 wins | 82 nominations	Budget = $1MM WWBO = $11MM D: The Weinstein Co. ISA: Hyde Park Ent. In Theaters: 16 weeks Widest Release: 450 Logline 7 wins | 43 Nominations (1 Oscar)

2007	2002
Budget = $150K U.S. B.O. = $9.4 MM D: FOX Searchlight ISA: Summit Widest Release: 150 16 weeks in theaters Logline 1 Academy Award | 21 wins | 26 nominations	Budget = $20M U.S. B.O = $56M P/D: Fox 2000 Pictures Widest Release: 1,836 20 weeks in theaters Logline 12 nominations

Sample Creative & Marketing Comp List: Ultra-Low Budget, Gritty Rock Drama

Under the Tuscan Sun
2003 | 1h 53m | PG-13 | Comedy, Drama, Romance
★6.8 ☆ Rate 52 Metascore
Audrey Wells | Diane Lane, Raoul Bova, Sandra Oh
A writer impulsively buys a villa in Tuscany in order to change her life.

Year of the Comet
1992 | 1h 31m | PG-13 | Action, Adventure, Romance
★5.8 ☆ Rate
Peter Yates | Penelope Ann Miller, Tim Daly, Louis Jourdan
An extremely rare bottle of wine (bottled during the appearance of the Great Comet of 1811) is discovered. Margaret Harwood is sent to retrieve it so it can be sold at auction. Oliver Plexico is assigned as her travel...

A Good Year
2006 | 1h 57m | PG-13 | Comedy, Drama, Romance
★7.0 ☆ Rate 47 Metascore
Ridley Scott | Russell Crowe, Abbie Cornish, Albert Finney
A British investment broker inherits his uncle's chateau and vineyard in Provence, where he spent much of his childhood. He discovers a new laid-back lifestyle as he tries to renovate the estate to be sold.

Bottle Shock
2008 | 1h 50m | PG-13 | Comedy, Drama
★6.8 ☆ Rate 56 Metascore
Randall Miller | Chris Pine, Alan Rickman, Bill Pullman
The story of the early days of California wine making featuring the now infamous, blind Paris wine tasting of 1976 that has come to be known as "Judgment of Paris".

Sample Creative & Marketing Comp List: Wine Comedy Romance

IMDb can also be mined to search via plot keywords. Right below "Storyline," you should see "Plot Keywords" (right above "Taglines"). If you click on "See All," you can then click on any plot keyword that your project has in common — and all the other projects that have that keyword as well (or share a series of them) will populate the list. This list can be sorted a number of ways (alphabetically, by popularity, release year, etc.) and narrowed down even further by genre(s) and/or delineating between film and TV (episodes, TV movie, mini-series, etc.).

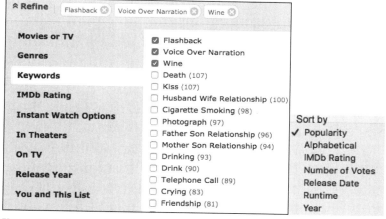

Use multiple keywords and sort options to search for comps on IMDb.

Digging around in this way, you might find comps you've never even heard of. This can be invaluable if you're struggling to find recent or good financial comps or even creative ones to brainstorm story problems.

Pinterest, Evernote, OneNote and other internet discovery and capture apps can be used to collect, curate and share research and visual information. Right click and save the posters of comps. Add their loglines and taglines in the comments section. Make a board of the headshots of your cast or the actors on your wish list — especially images that most look like how you envision them as your characters. Add their most relevant credits. Post images of prospective or representative locations or the cinematic styles or even music to consider adding to your look book. This can serve as a virtual filing cabinet of relevant research articles on the industry, subject matter or even prospects. These boards or notebooks can be used privately for internal development, to collaborate with a far-flung team, or even publicly as a portal for social media efforts such as key art or cast voting or even fan-submitted meme or clip competitions.

Studying how your comps — both successes and failures — were marketed can be very telling. *What do they have in common?* List and analyze these elements. *Notice any patterns?* Brainstorm taglines. *What is it you like (or don't like) about their marketing campaigns? What is similar — or different — from your film? Do most of the thriller comps have a gun and a running lead in the trailer? Is there always blood in the poster of the horror comps? Do all the romances highlight both leads?* Sometimes we miss the obvious.

This is a great exercise to do at any stage — and repeatedly — throughout the entire development and marketing processes. Breaking it all down can reveal if your project is really a different genre — or might be better served in a different genre — than you originally thought. Reviewing all these comps might make you reconsider where your project fits in the marketplace.

COMP RESEARCH RESOURCES

- AFI.com/100years
- Amazon
- IMDb.com
- IMSDB.com (scripts)
- Itcher.com
- Movie-Map.com
- Netflix
- Pro.IMDb.com
- Rotten Tomatoes
- TasteDive.com
- TheMovieDb.org (also TV)
- TV.com
- WhatIsMyMovie.com
- Wikipedia

Financial Comps

Financial comps are the most common because they are the easiest to identify. They are black-and-white, historical statistics. Perhaps for this exact reason, they might also be the least relevant. It's a bit like script readers, whose only feedback is on formatting. Yes, of course, that's all important — but it objectifies art when there's so much more to consider. (But no one ever defended Hollywood as being innocent of objectification!) Still, for business plans, some equity investors will focus exclusively on your comps' stats. So, do your due diligence to make sure they are as germane as possible.

Like comparable homes used in a real estate appraisal to establish a home's fair market value for a home mortgage, financial comps should be as current as possible, ideally within the last year or at least the last decade. Five years is reasonable and common. They should have the same caliber of cast you have attached or can reasonably secure.

They should be as close as possible to your film's projected budget. This can be a challenge at any budget but strive to keep your spread reasonable: within ten million in the upper ranges and within a couple hundred thousand in the lower-budgeted indie arena. The Screen Actors Guilds' groupings are a solid matrix[4] to adhere to. Use only SAG Low Budget films if you're under $2.5M. Gather under-$700K references if you're producing a Modified Low Budget project. Stick to SAG's Ultra Low Budget comparisons if you're under $200K.

Your financial comps should ideally be of the exact same genre or close subgenres. A dark horror comedy targets quite a different audience than a family comedy or straight horror. If you can't find "close enough" genre comps, then bracket your subgenres so you cross-collateralize to somewhat unskew your average.

---

[4] Visit my website, *HeatherHale.com* for my Unions' Low Budget Contracts Matrix.

Business plans or proposals might compare MPAA ratings (G, PG, PG-13, R, NC-17), runtime, director bankability, star marquee value, award wins and nominations and other categories. DVD sales statistics can be expensive or difficult to acquire and it's nearly impossible to get accurate figures out of the streaming behemoths (Netflix and Amazon) because they don't have to disclose this data to anyone. They don't have any advertisers to defend ad rates to, so their nonlinear "ratings" (how many downloads and views) are nobody's business but their own.

It's tough to quantify commercial art via calculating averages and medians. While reducing comp lists to some standard-deviation formula might pencil out nicely mathematically, it'll likely mean nothing in the reel world. But you know your comps better than anyone. Trust that. Own your subject matter expertise. You should be able to viscerally omit the outliers to create a more relevant bell curve. You won't likely have to defend this rationale because the calculations will all have been made after this curation. Thus, depending on the quantity and quality of your comp list, tossing out the top and bottom 3%–10% might yield the most realistic predictions.

FILM & TV STATISTICAL RESEARCH SOURCES

BFI.org.UK	Studio System
Box Office Mojo	UNESCO
IMDb	Variety Insight
IMDbPro	Wikipedia
MPAA	
Nielsen	Google "the trades": [5]
The Numbers	• *Cynopsis*
Pew Research	• *Deadline Hollywood*
Screen Australia	• *The Hollywood Reporter*
Statista	• *IndieWire*
StephenFollows.com	• *Variety*
	• *The Wrap*

[5] "The trades" refers to entertainment industry-specific news sources.

"And . . . ACTION!"
Template to Begin Your Comp List

EXERCISE: Make a list of all your comps. This is an ongoing process. It can be a simple handwritten list on a legal pad, a word processing table or even a Pinterest board, but my favorite is a sortable spreadsheet. Something like the examples on the following page.

Templates can be downloaded for free off this book's companion website: *HeatherHale.com/StorySelling*. If you aren't analyzing a specific project, consider working through this exercise using your favorite movies or television shows (especially those in the same genres you write) because it might reveal things to you about your own sensibilities. If you're a writer with no intention of producing your project yourself, the financial info might feel like overkill but as long as you're in IMDb or Googling, if the info is right in front of you, you might as well plug that in, too, because data can reveal surprising patterns. Take the time to note significant awards nominations or wins (Oscars, Emmys, Golden Globes, BAFTAs, WGA, People's Choice — even Razzies). If TV, add specific episode titles and where they fall in the show (i.e., pilot, season #/episode #).

If you used spreadsheet software, sort the table every which way looking for patterns. Highest grossing or rated projects is an obvious, helpful view, but look at the group by MPAA ratings or critics' rankings. *Are there any production companies or distributors that dominate the list? What about directors or actors? Do you see any budget or box office trends? Is there a consistent number of weeks in cinemas? Average minutes? Is yours in the range? Any outliers? What about the key art? Recognize any common elements?*

Your Film Project's Title

Film Comp Title	Year	Genre(s)	Runtime	Key Art	Logline	Tagline(s)	Production Company	Distributor	Rating	Budget	Gross D.B.O.	W.W.B.O.	Max # of Screens	# of Weeks in Theaters	MetaCritic	Awards
Black Panther	2018	Action Adventure	134 min		T'Challa, heir to the hidden but advanced kingdom of Wakanda, must step forward to lead his people into a new future and must confront a challenger from his country's past.	Long live the king. Hero. Legend. King. A king will rise. The Avengers have a new king. All hail the king. Respect the Throne.	Marvel Studios	Walt Disney Studios Motion Pictures	PG-13	$200,000,000	$700,059,566	$1,347,071,259	4,020	23	80	20 wins 40 noms

Your TV Project's Title

TV Project Comp Title	Pilot Release Date - Last (Current)	Format & Genre(s)	Runtime	Key Art	Logline(s)	Tagline(s)	Studio (or Production Company)	Distributor (Original Broadcast, Cable or Streaming Network)	Rating	Budget	# of Seasons	# of Episodes	MetaCritic	Awards
Game of Thrones	4/17/2011 - 2019	One-Hour Drama / Action Adventure Drama	57 min		Series Logline: Nine noble families fight for control over the mythical lands of Westeros while an ancient enemy returns after being dormant for thousands of years. Pilot Logline: Jon Arryn, the Hand of the King, is dead. King Robert Baratheon plans to ask his oldest friend, Eddard Stark, to take Jon's place. Across the sea, Viserys Targaryen plans to wed his sister to a nomadic warlord in exchange for an army.	Winter is coming. When you play the game of thrones, you win or you die. The Game Begins War is Coming Five Kings. One Throne. All Men Must Die Justice Has a Price The Real War Is Between the Living and the Dead Winter is Here	HBO	HBO	TV-MA	Typical $10M/ep Final 6 $15M/Ep	8	S1 = 10 eps S2 = 10 eps S3 = 10 eps S4 = 10 eps S5 = 10 eps S6 = 10 eps S7 = 7 eps S8 = 8 eps	80	294 wins 490 noms E-W-ODS 2018, 2016, 2015 E-N-ODS 2014, 2013, 2012, 2011 E-W-OWDS all by DB&DBW S7E7: The Dragon and the Wolf* (2018) S6E9: Battle of the Bastards (2016) S5E10: Mother's Mercy (2015) S4E10: The Children (2014) S1E9: Baelor DB&DBW (2011) GG-N-BTVD 2017, 2016, 2015, 2012

CORE DEVELOPMENT & MARKETING COMPONENTS

Some screenwriters hate creating marketing materials. And pitching. Producers have to present their product in its best light to all strategic prospects. If you have an active, engaged agent and/or manager, or are affiliated with a production company with an in-house art and marketing department, or are a proven-profitable genius, you might not ever have to write anything other than scripts. A-list screenwriters' ideas and expertise are trusted because they are proven.

But the rest of us have to execute the idea on the page to demonstrate our skills and the promise of our projects in order to initiate or maintain sales and production momentum. Have you written a brilliant spec feature screenplay? Or an innovative pilot script? Do you have a fantastic idea for a reality TV show? Or are you compelled to create a documentary? Maybe you already have a completed film in the can — or a book you've authored that you'd like to see adapted to film or television. *What now?*

Q: What marketing materials should I have to pitch my project?

Ask ten executives this question, get a dozen answers. There is no definitive formula, no "one size fits all" solution. Actually, there is a correct answer. And it's actually the same secret answer for everything in Hollywood (*shhh. . .*): "It depends." It's contingent upon where you're at in your career and in the development of the project, what else is going on in the world and in the industry in particular.

Some proven, marquee-value names can sell a concept in the room off merely a verbal pitch because their track record backs them up. You'll hear stories in the trades and on panels of talented (and lucky) neophytes who wrote a particularly promising original pilot script. Sometimes birth-lottery nepotism got them paired by the developing studio or network with an appropriate short-listed showrunner who took the project straight to series — likely landing the newbie a powerful agent in the process. All that's great.

But if you're an unrepped writer, an independent producer or content creator, your success is going to be dependent on more practical realities: the quality of your writing and multi-media marketing skills, the financial resources you have or can attract, your ability to activate your network (and those of others) and — let's be honest — your discipline, dedication and hard work.

Regardless, for everyone and for all projects: The more effective your marketing materials, the better they can support the project and all the players at each phase of its development. The perpetual back and forth development-marketing-pitch zig-zag — while frustrating, *hopefully* improves the script, format or intellectual property with every new iteration. All that prep-aration and practice empowers you to deliver better pitches — and exponentially improves and accelerates the develop-ment of future projects.

You'll need at least a one sheet for most projects (a logline and a summary or synopsis). Usually, you need a literary asset to sell (the script or TV format) but projects have been sold off verbal pitches with beat outlines or treatments.

The majority of the most common marketing elements and deliverables follow, detailed in one (but not the only) logical building order. As you progress, they build upon one another. As you become more proficient, they will all get easier and you might be able to skip some steps.

Both film and television, fiction and nonfiction are addressed, as the principals of story*telling* and story*selling* are universal. Understanding their overlapping structure and simi-lar goals will empower you to refine what will best serve each of your projects.

Let's start with the spine of all of them:

The Crucial Logline

The importance of great loglines to the development, marketing and pitching processes cannot be over-emphasized. Your logline is the lynchpin to your success. No matter what you're pitching, to whom, where or how — your pitch should always start with a fantastic logline.

Loglines tell prospective readers or viewers what this script, novel, movie, TV series, episode or chapter of the franchise is about. They distill the 10,000-foot bird's-eye view of your overall concept. These are the brief write-ups in streaming menus. They are the core of the infamous thirty-second elevator pitch.

Loglines capture the essence of a story. High-concept plots pique interest while meaningful themes add resonance. Completely self-contained, loglines are the single most important selling tool for your projects (save being fully funded with A-list attachments, a family member who owns a studio, or winning the lottery).

Loglines Are the Reduction Sauce of Your Project

If you're a foodie or a cook, you likely know what a reduction sauce is. It can be a sweet sauce, drizzled over a dessert, or a savory gravy, dolloped over a protein or vegetable. Either way, it starts as this huge tureen of raw ingredients and is slowly boiled down into this rich, dense, fully saturated, unified flavor, "reducing" everything to its core essence. Like a Broadway or operatic overture revealing snippets of the music and moods to come, loglines are an alluring tease, a synthesis of the essential elements but with their own unique structure.

Not surprisingly, all of the fundamentals critical to writing a terrific logline are the same for writing a solid script or editing a fantastic piece of content, which is why reverse-engineering back and forth enhances both. One informs and improves the other in a constantly shifting dance.

But it all starts and ends with the logline, the overarching idea. Loglines illuminate the concept's spine. They light the runway. If your logline isn't working, it's more than likely reflecting problems inherent in your script.

LOGLINE ETYMOLOGY

Originally a nautical term, "loglines" were long ropes with knots tied at consistent intervals weighted down by a wooden "chip log" panel at the end. Mariners in the 1500s unreeled these lines behind their ships to measure their speed. The faster the ship sailed, the faster the rope unwound. Thirty-second hourglasses measured "knots," the original nautical speed unit.

Early Hollywood story departments would "log" scripts in by writing the title and a succinct, one-line summary on the spine of the screenplay, on the title page and in their logbooks to track readers' assignments, development status, production and marketing inventory.

Logline Job Description

A logline's primary purpose is to entice interest in a project and inspire action. To get someone to read a script. Or buy a pitch. To stimulate audiences to buy a movie ticket or click to watch.

Loglines should emulate the viewing experience. Listeners or readers should be able to see the movie or television show unfold in their mind's eye; be thrilled by the spectacle, amused by the comedy or wince at the horror.

Loglines save everyone time. At a glance, everyone in the process can assess if this matches their sensibilities, is what they're looking for, what they can afford to pull off — and most importantly: what they can turn around and sell — internally up the ladder — or externally to market to prospective audience members.

Loglines help writers brainstorm new story concepts and serve as a guide to keep them focused on the core elements as they write (and rewrite and rewrite). Loglines lead off your query letters to help you get your project in front of producers, agents and managers. They launch your pitches to help you sell your screenplays, yourself as a writer, your projects, or you as a producer.

Loglines wear a lot of hats and have to do a lot of heavy lifting throughout the entire development process. A great logline can even last the entire length of the marketing cycle. The people you're pitching to use your logline to assess whether or not they might be interested in reading the entire literary asset or viewing your content (or assigning either to someone else). They give decision-makers a glimpse of how they might be able to turn around and sell it to their own decision-makers and stakeholders.

The most important question you'll be asked in the sales process is: *What's the logline?* (Or *What's your script/project about?*). Great loglines open doors, create working relationships and help get projects made. The significance and importance to your career success of these simple little sentences cannot be overestimated. The better you can get at writing them, the more you increase your odds of success.

WIIFM?

Like any other sales activity, your listener or reader is looking for: _What's in it for me?_ WIIFM? In show business, your art becomes a commodity, a widget to sell. Painful as that may be for an artist to accept, if you want to sell, you're gonna have to focus on what's in it for *them. What are the benefits? What do they get out of it? Not* what you put into it.

As screenwriters or authors, filmmakers or content creators, we are profoundly aware of how much genuine intention and earnest hard work went into developing our literary material or producing our finished assets, but the hard, painful truth you have to accept is: *nobody cares*. I know that's a tough truth to hear (I have to remind myself of it *every day*). *We* care about how we came up with the idea, its backstory and influences. We're delighted to share our clever solutions to every problem. But no one else cares (except maybe your precious writers' group who keeps you sane — bless them!). Save it for your panel at The Austin Film Fest where they truly revere and cherish writers. But to get there — for now (I hate to be the one to point it out, but...): *Let it go*. And never lose sight of WIIFM? Because that's all anyone else cares about, at every step of the process, regardless of budget level, genre, target audience. *What's in it for them?*

Unique Selling Point

You want your project to stand out from the crowd. In advertising, they refer to this as your USP, your u̲nique s̲elling p̲oint. This is what sets your project apart from all your competitors'. Your logline must convey — simply, elegantly, and above all, quickly — what it is about your film or TV show that will compel your target audience to pay to view: to ticket or click it.

Unfortunately, like an audition or a reel, a logline may simply provide a knee jerk excuse to say "No." To swipe left. To simply delete a junk email query or drag an unsolicited SPAM one sheet into the trash. Your screenplay's entire future — or at least its first chance at getting read or appreciated (not to mention eventually bought or made) — is completely reliant on your logline being compelling enough to even begin the sales process. And it only gets exponentially magnified after that.

If you've ever been to a film or TV market, you have probably been overwhelmed by the mind-boggling amount of competition that's there. It's hard enough handing out one sheets for your finished projects, but pitching concepts still in development can be quite intimidating. But that's nothing compared to trying to attract consumer eyeballs in the chaotic din that our modern global media landscape has become.

You invested months — probably years — in your project. Don't handicap it by dashing off a "placeholder" logline that'll "do for now," then beat yourself up because no one is intrigued enough by that shoddy effort to bother to read your script or take a meeting with you. Do your project — and yourself — a favor: Be as conscientious about your logline and marketing materials as you are about your script. Or hire someone to write an awesome one for you.

WHO READS LOGLINES?

- Studio Executives
- A-List Stars
- Producers
- Financiers
- Ad Agencies
- Brands
- Agents
- Entertainment Attorneys
- Network Executives
- Directors
- Distributors
- Investors
- Advertisers
- Publishers
- Managers
- Audience Members

Who Doesn't?

Loglines are read by virtually everyone in the entertainment industry or anyone interested in its properties. Producers, agents and managers may use your original logline to pitch "their" (now) project to studios, networks, stars, directors, financiers and distributors. Loglines help keep all the department heads on the same page so everyone's actually making the same movie or television show. International sales agents may use this same logline on their one sheets to sell the movie or television show to foreign distributors in different territories at the markets. Exhibitors and festivals may use that same logline to advertise the movie to local theater audiences via newspapers and programs. Broadcasters and networks may use it online and in magazines. It may even make its way to the upfronts to pitch ad agencies to turn around and convince their brands to invest in these television shows. Distributors and retailers may use it on the back of the DVDs. Prospective audience members use loglines to decide if they are willing to commit the money and time to pay to watch the content — or get someone to watch it with them. Virtually every IMDb, Variety Insight or Rotten Tomatoes project entry has at least one logline listed (and sometimes several). All the industry box office and business sites use them as well as all those direct-to-consumers.

"The best script is one that never has to be read."

I know that is anathema to most writers. But it's so hard to get people in "Hollywood" (i.e., anywhere in the global media marketplace) to read scripts. "No one has time." But if you had a silver bullet — a high-concept logline that was so good, it could shoot your script through all the decision-makers in the chain, past all those who might not appreciate the read anyway, those who will never even get to it and will just bog the whole process down for months to years — and land in the bull's-eye of your greenlighter's signature pen... wouldn't you use it?

Your logline is your silver bullet.

Scripts are meant to be shot. Keep your eye on the goal. It's so worth your time and effort to get better and better at crafting these critical gems.

Logline Construction

Like everything else in the entertainment industry, constructing effective and compelling loglines is part art, part craft. Art is memorable, visceral, intuitive, magical. Craft, if done well, is virtually invisible to anyone not accustomed to actually looking for it (but obvious — in a confidence-endearing way — to those who are).

Pros debate the length of loglines. Some mandate thirty-five words. Some sticklers urge just twenty-five *max*. Some'll grant you two sentences. The industry standard is just one (thus, their "one-liner" nickname). Let's just agree that it should be as short as it can possibly be. Never waste a word.

An arbitrary but simple starting place to begin to develop your logline is to create a single sentence with three elements as a baseline: subject, verb, direct object. Try starting with the title and the genre straight off the bat to orient your listener.

[*Title*] is a [Genre/Format] about. . .

Something like:[1]

- ○ *Breaking News* is a contained thriller about. . .
- ○ *The Undetected* is a one-hour drama about. . .
- ○ *3D Cakes* is an ensemble, culinary reality build show that tracks. . .

Then anchor the bearing walls:

1. **Subject** = Protagonist (main character or ensemble)
2. **Verb** = Battle (obstacle/goal/conflict/moral dilemma)

---

[1] NOTE: None of the examples shared in this book are presented as perfect. They are merely real-world works-in-progress (constantly being rewritten, too) to help illustrate this process.

3. **Direct Object** = Antagonist (antagonistic force/stakes)

- The **subject** of this one-sentence logline — at least for features and scripted television — will usually describe an imperfect, passionate but hopefully proactive protagonist. You may prefer to call her a flawed main character or it may be actually an ensemble (a team or a group) — whatever — the lead driving the action.
- The **verb** of our sentence will depict the battle, the obstacle or conflict — all the better if it's a moral dilemma.
- The **direct object** may describe an insurmountable antagonist who stands in the way of the protagonist or tries to stop the main character or ensemble from reaching his/her/their goal. Ideally, this is a big, clear, physical, cinematic target that we can visualize him or her pursuing — and imagine the stakes that hang in the balance.

[Title] is a [genre/format] about [an interesting, proactive protagonist] who wants to/must [protagonist's goal/battle] but [stakes/conflict] (what stands in the way or happens if the protagonist fails?).

Malibu Wishes is a sitcom about a Jim Cramer–like financial wizard who is ruined in a Madoff scandal and must convert his Malibu mansion into a celebrity rehab in order to save it from foreclosure.

The 6 Qs = The Spine of Your Logline

As we discussed in the Introduction, one simple way to build your logline is to use the six questions journalists have used since the beginning of news to tell a story: *Who, What, Where, When, Why* and *How*. This inverted pyramid inherently forces you to stay focused on the top notes, the most important elements of your story. Start with the most compelling, newsworthy or freshest information first before funneling down into the rest of your pitch.

Your logline is your ad copy and may include some combination of the following:

NOTE: **Bold** = Critical

Italics = It depends on the project

WHO

- **is the main character? (protagonist)**
- *stands in his or her way? (antagonist)*

WHAT

- **happens to him or her? (catalyst/inciting incident)**
- **does she or he want? (goal)**
- **is the problem/conflict? (obstacles/stakes)**
- *is the most important moment in the script? (climax)*

WHERE/WHEN is the story set? (storyworld)

HOW does the main character. . .

- overcome adversity? (plot)
- evolve psychologically (transformational character arc)
- *resolve the conflict? (HOW the story ends)*

WHY we should care? (theme)

Essential Logline Elements

TITLE

A great title is the leadoff marketing asset. Ideally, your title conjures the genre. Sometimes it'll eponymize the protagonist, milieu, plot, stakes or even the theme. Like your logline, it's possible it could stay with the project all the way through to the home audience.

Sometimes your title makes your genre really obvious, but you want to make sure your listener or reader is clear on your intent. You don't want them laughing at your horror story or thinking your thriller is a dark comedy. Think of your genre as an establishing shot: You're letting them know where we're at.

If — *when!* — your script sells or your project gets set up, it's quite possible (even likely) that your title may change many times over. And even though you probably won't get to pick your title (or it won't stick), you still need to have a working title. And of course, as with everything else, it has to be excellent. Ask anyone who reads your script or hears your practice pitches to offer up suggestions. Keep a running list of alternates you like. Often, the best title will be buried somewhere in the script.

Knowing they'll ultimately be changed, some screenwriters and producers pitch with titles they know could never be advertised just to entertain industry insiders and generate internal buzz and heat.

 INDUSTRY SHOPPING TITLE EXAMPLES

American Pie was originally titled: *Untitled Teenage Sex Comedy That Can Be Made for Under $10 Million That Most Readers Will Probably Hate But I Think You Will Love*
Friends With Benefits, Justin Timberlake and Mila Kunis's Rom-Com, was originally titled *F*ckbuddies.*
New Girl's 8-page pitch document read, "The working title of the show is *Chicks and Dicks.* But obviously this isn't France, so we'll have to change it."

 REAL WORLD TITLE CHANGE EXAMPLES

Writers rarely have a say in marketing. The title of my original spec script, *Quadroon Ball,* set the time and place (mid-1800s New Orleans), revealed it'd be a costume period piece and hinted at the racial, gender and other socioeconomic cultural issues it'd contend with. Lifetime retitled it to *The Courage to*

Love which I found ironically counterintuitive because that was the antithesis of both the plot and theme. The protagonist, Henriette Díaz DeLille, played by Vanessa Williams, had to find the courage to *not* love. She had to forsake at least her romantic love and paternal love to stand in faith and integrity. Perhaps their argument was for a greater love — to become the first African American nun ever ordained by the Catholic Church (and possibly soon the first African American saint).

The title of our ultra-low budget thriller *Witness Insecurity* was originally a play on the faith-based "witnessing" element set against a backdrop of the witness protection program. The first distributor changed the title to *Snitch*. But that then competed with a much bigger-budgeted Dwayne "The Rock" Johnson release. The second distributor changed the title to *Absolute Killers*, I'm sure so the "Ab" would rank it atop the alphabetical streaming and pay-per-view guides.

Sometimes it can be effective to end with your title, especially if you can "ba-dump-bump!" it into the sentence. If your title is also the name of the secret society, the code name for the heist, the cure for the viral outbreak or the ultimate reward/award, it might be nice to end with that as the last thing they hear (or read):

[Antagonist] ... [Protagonist] ... [Verb] ... [Goal] ... [Stakes] ... [Title].

Terrorists bomb-rig the car of a high school football coach and force him to be a suicide bomber. To save his family and his country, he must make it from coast to coast in *21 Hours*.

TAGLINE

Taglines can help flesh out the image the logline paints, adding a funny or foreboding ironic twist. Taglines are all understood within the context of their title and understood in an instant when accompanied by their key art.

TAGLINE EXAMPLES

12 Monkeys The future is history.
Alien In space, no one can hear you scream.
Brokeback Mountain Love is a force of nature.
Chicken Run Escape or die frying.
Contagion Nothing spreads like fear.
Deliverance This is the weekend they didn't play golf.
Greedy Where there's a will, there's a relative.

I Am Legend The last man on earth is not alone.

Jaws 2 Just when you thought it was safe to go back in the water.
Napoleon Dynamite He's out to prove he's got nothing to prove.
Platoon The first casualty of war is innocence.
Psycho Check in. Unpack. Relax. Take a Shower.
Quiz Show Fifty million people watching and no one saw a thing.
The 40-Year-Old Virgin The longer you wait, the harder it gets.
The Royal Tenenbaums Family isn't a word. It's a sentence.
The Social Network You don't get to 500 million friends without making a few enemies.
The Truman Show On the air. Unaware.
Tommy Boy If at first you don't succeed, lower your standards.
True Lies When he said I do, he never said what he did.

GENRE

Leading off with genre is always a smart way to start. It's the establishing shot of your logline, pitch or query. Genre telegraphs structure and audience demographics, projects budget and potential revenue and orients your reader or listener to sensibilities and scope. Just keep in mind the expectations of your genre — and satisfy them.

If you did the comp spreadsheet exercise and studied how similar projects were marketed to their respective audiences, you should have a pretty good idea of your genre, genres or subgenres. Playing with your logline with that new palette might make you realize one genre is clearly more marketable than another and that might be a better promotional angle. Remember: The goal is to get them to read the script.

Refine Your Genre Beyond "Just" Drama

I'm sure you've heard: "Dramas don't sell." But all storytelling is drama. Drama is conflict. Drama is performed action. Moving images are produced to move audiences. Both fiction and nonfiction films as well as scripted and unscripted television programming share common DNA: They're all drama (or at least they should be). So, it's an oxymoron to say: "Dramas don't sell!" because it's all drama.

That said, straight dramas are, without a doubt, the toughest, most customized films and television shows to market because there are an infinite number of variables.

Drama can be murky to market. Drama audiences are hard to discern and they aren't really transferable from one project to the next. It's difficult to parlay the traction of one stand-alone story to another. Without any genre-specific language or images to fall back on, distributors must start from scratch each time. Try to be more genre-specific than just the generic "Drama" in your pitch.

But dramas are what many feature screenwriters want to write, what many independent filmmakers and content creators want to shoot and, fortunately, what many stars want to attach to. And stars attract audiences. Quality content attracts talented, high-profile actors who in turn attract talented department heads who want to participate in meaningful material. All of this entices and raises the communal bar on the whole collaborative enterprise. Well-written dramas are magnets that lure the necessary critical mass to reach that elusive tipping point.

Provided your project delivers on the promise of its potential, the snowballing momentum of an excellent literary blueprint, brilliantly cast against terrific production values, will engage the right distributors and sales agents to commit to your project and your content may find its audience. If a drama is done exceedingly well (and can find and connect with its audience), it can enjoy an outsize share of prestige and momentum and sometimes even profit! The one place dramas perform better than any other genre is at major festivals, so if you're squarely in that space, your marketing campaign strategy is pretty obvious.

While drama is the lifeblood of passionate indie films — and the television renaissance we're enjoying around the globe — the difficulty of selling it is one of the many reasons (albeit a lazy one) for the glut of sequels, prequels and reboots of old TV shows as feature films or classic movies retooled as new television shows or clones licensed and translated from one territory to another (e.g., *Les Revenants/The Returned*).

Studios love to adapt bestselling novels, beloved comic books — even spin-offs of Twitter feeds or amusement park rides — because they bank on the presumed pre-existing audience awareness of the underlying intellectual property. Sometimes blockbusters result, like *Harry Potter* and *Pirates of the Caribbean*; sometimes it backfires, like *The Lone Ranger*, *John Carter*, *Sahara*, *Speed Racer* and *Green Lantern*. But these greenlit commodities are usually genre-based: fantasy, adventure, thriller, science fiction, romance, erotica (*Fifty Shades of Grey*) — and thus more marketable.

Genre provides a gauge for budget and demographics. Genre classifications set audiences' expectations. Anthology series like *Black Mirror, American Horror Story* and *True Detective* are packaged seasons of a genre brand that keeps audiences coming back for more entertainment in that clearly delineated lane. Much like a cable channel, they cater to a specific audience who knows what to expect — and gets it, every time they tune in.

But drama is too broad a genre to pigeonhole. Audiences buy cinema tickets to comedies to laugh, click the remote to watch horror series to be scared, but all bets are off with dramas, which are often assumed to be serious (at the risk of being less entertaining). Anything that isn't clearly something else gets lumped in with drama. And they're difficult to sell.

It's infinitely easier to promote your project if you can lean your drama into a genre. Any genre. Some subgenres and genre combinations are easier to market than others. So, look for the aspects you can pitch: thrilling (thriller, horror, suspense); spectacular (action and adventure); and/or amusing (comedy, romantic comedy and musical) — great if it could hit all three.

Main Characters

Your logline should identify your main character. *Whose story is this? Which character are we meant to identify with and root for? Whose dynamic actions propel the story? Who is your hero?* Ideally, the leadoff characteristic you use to describe your protagonist will relate directly to the plot and the theme. This may be his or her first-impression trait or fatal flaw that drives the transformational arc. While your focus should be on precise nouns (i.e., identifying them by their specific vocation or relevant role), your use of adjectives is precious. Make sure the one you use is the most important one.

If it's an ensemble, of course you can use "a team/group of," but *does one character stand out or "arc" (i.e., change or evolve) more than the others? Are any of the characters the central focus of attention?* If it's a series, *whose motivations or actions launch the pilot? Lead this episode or chapter?*

Focus your logline on the central character driving the action in *this* story.

CHARACTER NAMES

It's not typically necessary to use character names in loglines because it could confuse your listener trying to keep track of so many details in such a dense sentence.

Exceptions include: if your protagonist is famous from history (Catherine the Great), or living-memory headlines (Tanya Harding, OJ Simpson), or if you're writing about characters the reader might already be familiar with (e.g., future episode loglines in a TV series pitch package or familiar franchise characters like James Bond or super heroes), or if the title integrates the character's name.

An easy, memorable shorthand to identify characters and help your pitch recipients keep track is simply through the characters' roles in the story, their relationship to the other characters, their current, former or aspirational vocations or interests — especially if these details are relevant — or (even better) diametrically opposed to their "call to action" in the story. For example: an ageing baseball player trains for an impossible comeback; an alcoholic commercial pilot must defend his miraculous crash landing; a homeless single parent fights for custody and new love, etc.

CHARACTER FLAWS

The character flaw called out in the logline usually telegraphs the character's transformational arc and serves as a metaphor for the theme. Every word in your logline should be a key factor in your story.

What happens in the plot might seem to be the worst thing that could possibly happen to a hero with that particular character flaw. But as it unfolds, it becomes clear it was the best thing that could've possibly happened because it forces them to grow out of their stagnant state and evolve into infinitely better versions of themselves.

Stories are plots that force the hero to grow. Plots show us who a character is by how they respond to major change. Whatever specific adjective you select to describe your protagonist's flaw is going to be assumed to be her greatest opportunity for emotional growth and that her "Hero's Journey" will stem from the plot challenge you designed that forces her to overcome that flaw to personify the project's theme.

OCCUPATION AND ROLE

High-concept hooks often rely on irony. The hero's occupation may starkly contrast her flaw or the opposite of what we expect is what actually unfolds. The first 10% of your story should cinematically illustrate your main character's flaws, tonally in keeping with the project's genre. If it's a comedy, establishing her world and her weaknesses should be funny. If it's a thriller, the setup should be exciting, suspenseful.

SAMPLE LOGLINE CHARACTER DESCRIPTORS

- disgraced politician
- Burundian refugee
- undercover ICE agent
- lapsed Catholic
- gluten-intolerant, diabetic baker
- sheriff with OCD
- Purple Heart recipient turned reality star
- therapist with Asperger's
- closeted medium
- schizophrenic dinosaur
- Amish astronaut
- Muslim feminist school teacher turned politician
- illiterate college graduate
- bronze medal–winning Paralympian

- assassin with Alzheimer's
- organ donor with AIDS
- double-amputee motivational speaker
- hippie rabbi
- vegan butcher
- selfish social worker
- cowardly trophy hunter
- materialistic teen
- womanizing pastor
- mother second-guessing she ever wanted kids

ACTION HEROES VS. THRILLER PROTAGONISTS

A key difference between the action and thriller genres is that an action hero is usually trained, well-equipped and eager to leap into battle whereas in a thriller, the protagonist is often an innocent caught up in something she doesn't understand and has to figure out, picking up the necessary skills, tools and allies on the fly. Your logline is the first chance to make this clear distinction by giving us a sense of who they are, what they're made of. . . and destined to become.

Lara Croft, Rambo, the Terminator, Batman, Superman (among hundreds of other examples) appear like action figures in a box: complete with built-in fighting expertise and specific weapons and vehicles that make them uniquely formidable to their respective opponents. Whereas reluctant heroes like Katniss Everdeen, Luke Skywalker, Rocky or the Karate Kid had to accept the mission that was thrust upon them and be mentored along the way to discover and develop their innate abilities and find their inner strength to persevere.

Interesting hybrid characters exist in the grey area between thriller and action, often explored through science fiction or graphic novels. Clones (*Resident Evil*) or AI

(*Extant, Humans*) struggle with their humanity and individuality in contrast to their genetic memories or operating systems. Sleeper agents such as Jason Bourne, who discovers he has instinctive muscle-memory skills while unraveling his own forgotten past, realizing he awakened, unconscious to his own volitional embedded triggers and orders. Or characters who were unwillingly made into monsters or superheroes; Frankenstein or *X-Men*'s Wolverine are fascinating entries along this spectrum.

CATALYST & INCITING INCIDENT

Every story has a beginning, middle, and end, but it is not necessary to reveal all three in your logline. How, when and where you choose to come into your story — and get out of it — are part of your creative arsenal. But you must begin somewhere.

There is a lot of debate over the difference between a catalyst and an inciting incident. They are often confused, transposed, merged or renamed. Some stories suffer from starting too far back. Others are reminiscent of throat-clearing before speaking or trying to get an old engine to turn over, redundantly revving the same clutter noise over and over before actually getting going.

A catalyst is an agent that causes an event whereas an inciting incident is an event that provokes change. The difference is subtle.

The catalyst may be passive; it may have occurred in the past or offscreen. But it *causes* the inciting incident, which triggers the central problem of the story. The catalyst *motivates* the protagonist's *reaction* to the inciting incident — which is where the story officially "starts." The catalyst is the result of the backstory that probably led to your character's developing the flaw that she will likely have to overcome as the internal obstacle in this movie or television episode.

The inciting incident is the new opportunity that launches your character into her new situation. It's what sets the story in motion and gives her the opportunity to change her future. Thus, you want to get to your inciting incident as quickly as possible.

As your logline is the distillation of your story, it'd be quite difficult to construct one without "what happens" (the inciting incident) or what happened (how we got here, what motivates the quest: the catalyst).

Thus, you have your setup: a character with a problem, a dilemma stemming from the past catalyst. The plot of each story is launched by its inciting incident — the predicament that disrupts and alters your character's life and sets this story in motion.

GOAL

Your protagonist should proactively pursue a plot-realized goal. As this drives your entire story, it should be made clear early in your script. It should also drive your logline. And your logline should pay off early in the read. The moment your script reader concedes that your project doesn't live up to the promise of its pitch, she may stop reading the script. And there crashes all the momentum of your successful pitch.

What is the quest? What does your main character want? What is the overarching external goal that will drive the events of the second act and keep on escalating straight through the third act driving to the climax? (e.g., protect the children, blow up the bad guys, rescue the prince, find the groom, steal the MacGuffin, get the girl/guy/job, etc.).

THE MACGUFFIN

It's a plot device. It's whatever everyone is after. Especially in thrillers, where there is some sort of ticking clock.

Examples
- The antidote
- The Holy Grail
- The Maltese Falcon
- The flash drive with...
- The briefcase containing...
- The work of art everyone's chasing.
- The priceless bottle of wine with the fountain of youth on the label.

For audiences to care, the hero has to have a very strong motivation. One audiences can empathize with, even better if they can relate to it personally, viscerally. *What happens if your hero doesn't achieve their goal?* The more significant the consequences, the better.

Drama is all about conflict so we need to understand why this quest is going to be so difficult for *this* hero — and why it's so important *to her* — and why it promises to be fascinating to watch.

And what's at stake?

STAKES

Your logline needs to convey what's at stake. Loglines don't always include the antagonist because sometimes the antagonist is implied by the stakes.

Always look for the source of conflict in the story. *Who or what must the protagonist beat to achieve his or her goal or desired object? What makes the hero's quest impossible?* Obstacles and stakes are essential elements of conflict.

In a romantic comedy, the antagonist is often the love interest and the conflict is whatever is keeping them apart. In an action-driven piece, the conflict will be in the triangulation of the goal versus the stakes against the ticking clock. In a character-driven piece, the conflict will come from the situation she finds herself in or what she's confronted by (i.e., the outer conflict catalyzing her inner growth).

If you have created circumstances that accentuate a clearly defined central problem, perpetuating it from every angle but never actually solving it, then it is likely you have created the framework for a serialized TV show.

Nouns & Verbs

As is true of your screenplay, try to stick to just nouns and verbs as much as possible. There is precision in specificity. Only allow yourself to use adjectives or adverbs when they add a contrasting layer of depth.

The Power of Irony

The power of irony cannot be understated in a logline, especially for high-concept premises. Just like in comedy and horror, it is the gap between expectation and reality that makes people laugh or jump. Just as viewers like to add 2 + 2 for themselves to actively engage in solving the mystery or second-guessing the antagonist's plan, listeners to your pitch and readers of your logline enjoy figuring out the inherent conflict implied by the character arc that launches its inevitable climax.

Irony can be an especially great tool for rewriting backwards and forwards from logline to script — and back again, mining the collision subtext to explore untapped creative opportunities. The more elegant your execution, the more invisible your plot structure will be — but loglines illuminate the seams.

EXAMPLES OF LOGLINES USING IRONY

Jaws (1975) A local sheriff with a fear of the ocean must team up with a marine biologist and an old seafarer to hunt down a great white shark terrorizing a beach community.

Liar Liar (1997) A fast-talking lawyer and habitual liar can't tell a lie for 24 hours because of his son's birthday wish.

Miss Congeniality (2000) A tomboy FBI Agent must go undercover in the Miss United States beauty pageant to prevent a group from bombing the event.

KILL YOUR DARLING CLICHÉS

Phrases or expressions that have been used so often their original meaning has been diluted will make readers' eyes glaze right past them, ignoring what could likely be rewritten into a fresh observation. Uniquely and specifically describe exactly what you mean, or create a new symbolic metaphor that they have to unpack to discover for themselves.

But sometimes these tired, weak default phrases can be reinvigorated by toying with the language to make your audience see a play on the cliché with a fun, fresh meaning. Think of *Monsters, Inc.*'s "You won't believe your eye."

Logline Recipes

There is no magic formula. Formulas seem so dictatorial. Recipes tend to be more free-flowing and forgiving, allowing for more organic, customized creativity. Some of the most miraculous creations come from the collision of ideas. Just as you bring all that is uniquely you to your script, exercise all that same creativity with your logline. It is the first foot you put forward for your project.

There are as many logline templates to try out as there are screenwriting techniques. There's a lot of debate over the "right" way — just as there is seemingly endless debate over everything in Hollywood (and in the media. . . and on social media. . . and in politics. . . and in life). There are those who are convinced their system is the best (and many are great) and there are those who will ridicule any attempt to formalize the process. Some logline methods lend themselves better to one genre or format than others. And your preferences will likely evolve right along with your skills through the different phases in your career.

At the risk of overkill, I think it serves writers to canvass all their options. Play with all of them. Test different approaches.

Home in on what works best for you — on this specific project — which might be completely wrong for the tone or sensibilities of your next project. . . and rewrite and rewrite and rewrite. Focus group. Practice. And rewrite some more. Every single word changes many times, the order changes to test every conceivable nuance, which is why exercising your writing and pitching muscles with different kinds of stretches can prove so worthwhile. Like mind-mapping or improv, sometimes a string of laughably bad ideas can lead to a dramatic breakthrough.

The logline exercise that follows encourages you to try your hand at a variety of templates as a jumping-off place. One solid approach (especially if your script follows this model) is to use the industry standard language of The Hero's Journey, first broken down in Joseph Campbell's *Hero with a Thousand Faces*, then condensed and simplified for screenwriters (and the industry) by Christopher Vogler in his fine spin-off, *The Writer's Journey*. Another popular approach you might try is based on the beloved, late Blake Snyder's *Save the Cat!* theories and series. Logline templates based on his ten genres have been generously shared by Master Cat José Silerio, who served as Blake's development director. And everything the brilliant Michael Hauge teaches and writes should be employed. I noticed after writing this paragraph that all of these books were published by my new publisher: Michael Wiese Productions. I'm honored to be in such esteemed company.

 ## "And . . . ACTION!"
Logline Starting Place Worksheet

1. **Who** is your main character?

   a. Brainstorm 3–5 *really specific* adjectives describing him/her/them and *select one* (which may vary according to the other elements). Make sure to include their weakness/flaw, their catalyst or backstory, their function in the story (i.e., relationship to their vocation or the other characters — and how do they contrast with all?)

   b. How is he/she sympathetic?

2. **What** is she or he trying to accomplish?
3. **Who** or **what** stands in his/her/their way?
4. **What** is the story's first major event or inciting incident?
5. **What** happens if he/she/they fail(s)?
6. **What** makes this story unique?

"And . . . ACTION!"
Logline Brainstorming Exercises

Ever play *Mad Libs*? That fill-in-the-blank word game? Grab a pencil. Noodle around with these logline templates to brainstorm possible starting places for your project's logline. Feel free to change the order and every element to spin off variations of your own until you nail it (for now).

1. [Title] is a [Genre/Format] about [an interesting, proactive Protagonist] who wants to/must [Protagonist's Goal] but [Conflict/Stakes] *(stand in the way or happen if the Protagonist fails)*.

2. When [the Inciting Incident] occurs, [Hero] must [drive the Plot/pursue the Goal] before [Stakes] *occur.*

3. When [a major event happens], a [Specific Protagonist] must [Objective] or else [Stakes].

4. Once Upon a time there was [_____]. Every day, [_____]. One day, [_____]. Because of that, [_____]. Because of that, [_____]. Until finally [_____].[2]

5. Since [the Catalyst], [Main Character] hasn't been able to [Overcome Obstacle(s)/Character Flaw] but now he/she must [Pursue the Goal] or else [Stakes].

6. [Protagonist]. . .[Verb]. . .[Antagonist]. . .[Goal]. . . Stakes]. . .[Title].

---

[2] Google Pixar's 22 Rules of Storytelling.

CORE DEVELOPMENT & MARKETING COMPONENTS

7. [The Hero] [The Problem] [The Goal]. [Title].

8. When [a/the Flawed Hero] is forced to [Call to Adventure], (s)he must [Emotional Growth] or risk [Stakes].

9. [Hero] must overcome [Hero's Flaw] to pursue [Goal] or risk [Stakes].

10. A(n) [Adjective + Noun (Main Character)] who [wants/desires/dreams] to [possess/achieve/become something interesting] despite [critical opposition he or she faces].

11. When [the Inciting Incident happens], the [Main Character] must [complete the Goal] against a(n) [Antagonist's Flaw + Vocation/Role].

12. When [a major event happens], a(n) [Flaw + Main Character] must [overcome the Flaw] to [pursue the Goal].

13. When a [major event occurs], the [Protagonist's fatal flaw + vocation/role] must [dynamic Action] to overcome [Obstacle] or else [Stakes].

14. A [Main Character] must [Goal] to overcome [Problem/Obstacles/Flaw].

15. When a(n) [Adjective + Vocation/Role] tries to [Goal], [Antagonist/Obstacles]. . . [Title].

16. A [Protagonist] [Catalyst] *sets the story in motion* but now the [Obstacle] they must face [Stakes] [Goal].

17. My project is a [Genre/Format] called [Title] about a [Protagonist] who [is acted upon] but then [this happens], therefore he/she is forced to [do this] in order to [achieve/prevent this].

18. A [Protagonist] wants [Goal] despite [Obstacle], but if he/she doesn't *achieve* [Objective], [Stakes] *will occur.*

19. My project is a [Genre/Format] called [Title] about when [Inciting Incident *happens to*] a [Main Character] who wants/must [Goal/Objective] but/or else [Stakes].

That oughta get you started.

Test out your various loglines on friends and relatives. Heck, strangers. Pay attention to the words and phrases they repeat back to you (i.e., recall easily). *What are their questions? Where are they confused? What's most intriguing to them?* Pay attention to when they laugh. If they get confused.

Use your writers' group as a focus group. A bit like a table read, have another writer (or each of them) deliver variations on your loglines and you just watch their reactions and take notes. A great way to capitalize on a terrific writers' group is to ask all the writers to write loglines for every script they read. You're not asking them to do coverage — just a rough logline. Doesn't even have to be polished. They may be awful. They may blow yours away (sometimes a fresh set of eyes can be far more objective). There will likely be a few new keywords you hadn't considered or angles you haven't tried.

But *what did they think the story was about?* Good practice for them, too, but more importantly, you'll see a wide range of approaches that might illuminate what they thought your script was about versus what you thought it was. If all the loglines come back confusing, pitching a story you don't think you wrote, that's evidence that no one is getting the story you think you're telling, so you might need to revisit the seemingly perpetual rewriting phase.

Then let your reduction sauce simmer. Get away from it for a while. Just because your fingers aren't on the keyboard doesn't mean you're not writing. Sometimes you need to let what you've written — or the feedback — ferment in your subconscious awhile.

Then come back fresh — and prune it even pithier. Then take one more pass and trim it some more. Put it away and come back to it again and see if you can't hone it even more.

Loglines are rewritten constantly. Every word changed to test every conceivable nuance until you nail it. Like a chef, continually tasting and perfecting a sauce, you'll figure it out — and will likely refine it further with every presentation.

If you don't have a project in mind at the moment, still practice. Write loglines for your comps or favorite films or TV shows and — without revealing the titles — see if anyone can guess them.

BLAKE SNYDER'S *SAVE THE CAT!* LOGLINE TEMPLATE

The late great Blake Snyder revolutionized Hollywood thinking with his *Save the Cat!* series. Here is his logline template — and logline templates for his ten genres (if you're not familiar, read his MWP books). Special thanks to Blake's former development director, Master Cat José Silerio, for allowing us to include these for your practice.

On the verge of a [Statis/Death Moment] a [Flawed Protagonist] has a [Catalyst] and [Breaks Into Two] with the [B-Story] but when [MidPoint] happens, he/she must learn the [Theme] before the [All Is Lost Moment] to defeat the [Flawed Antagonist] (from getting away with his/her plan).

 ### "And . . . ACTION!" TEN *SAVE THE CAT!* GENRE LOGLINE TEMPLATES

Monster in the House: *Monster, House, Sin*
A *culpable* hero is forced to save a trapped group of people from being killed by a monster he inadvertently unleashed.

Golden Fleece: *Road, Team, Prize*
A *driven* hero must lead a group of allies to retrieve a prized possession through a perilous journey that wasn't what the hero expected.

Example: *Little Miss Sunshine* — When a dysfunctional family reluctantly embarks on a road trip to a "Little Miss" beauty pageant, they're forced to face their underlying problems and issues along the way or forever lose what truly matters most... each other.

Out of the Bottle: *Wish, Spell, Lesson*
A *covetous* hero must learn to undo a spell he wished for before it turns into a curse he can't undo.

Dude with a Problem: *Innocent Hero, Sudden Event, Life or Death*
An *unwitting* hero must survive at all costs when he is dragged into a life or death situation he never saw coming and cannot escape.

Rites of Passage: *Life Problem, Wrong Way, Acceptance*
A *troubled* hero's only way to overcome a spiraling life crisis is to defeat his worst enemy – himself.

Buddy Love: *Incomplete Hero, Counterpart, Complication*
An *inadequate* hero must rise above an extremely difficult situation to be with a uniquely unlikely partner who is the only one capable of bringing him peace.

Whydunit: *Detective, Secret, Dark Turn*
A *single-minded* hero must find the truth to an intriguing mystery before he is swallowed by the darkness he desperately seeks to expose.

Fool Triumphant: *Fool, Establishment, Transmutation*
An *innocent* hero's only way to defeat the prejudices of a group is to change himself without losing what made him the group's target of disdain in the first place — his uniqueness.

Institutionalized: *Group, Choice, Sacrifice*
An outsider's only way to save his individuality is by going against the many who wish to integrate him into their fold.

Example: *Zero Dark Thirty* — An unrelenting CIA operative must track down the elusive Osama Bin Laden as she risks all against his fanatical followers and her own bureaucratic agency.

Superhero: *Special Power, Nemesis, Curse*
A *uniquely special* hero must defeat an opponent with stronger capabilities by using the same powers that disconnect him from the people he hopes to save.

A great logline and a fantastic script are "all" a feature screenwriter should need to attract an agent, manager or producer. The rest of these deliverables are more focused on feature film producers and TV writers, but sometimes, if they like your logline and/or your query or your pitch, you might be asked for a synopsis (or your producer might ask you to help write the rest!).

Summary

A summary is what the story is about (top note, big picture) while a synopsis describes the story, beat by beat. They are both condensed versions of the literary material or media product.

There's often confusion as to the difference between a summary and a synopsis. If you look synopsis up in the dictionary, it reads: "summary." That's helpful. And a one sheet is two pages. Ah, Hollywood. . .

Lacking any definitive industry standard, let's just adhere to IMDb's current field parameters. At the time of printing, IMDb limits summaries to about one paragraph (up to 220 words) and synopses range from a couple of paragraphs up to two pages (239-word minimum to 936 words maximum).

HOW LONG SHOULD THEY BE?

For simplicity's sake, let's just ballpark:

Logline	=	1 Sentence
Summary	=	1 Paragraph
Synopsis	=	1 Page

Ballpark.

What you're using your summary for should influence it. Never lose sight of your audience or your end game. If the summary is for a business-to-consumer (B2C) promotion, such as

IMDb, Rotten Tomatoes (which populates from IMDb) or WithoutaBox (what most festivals will import from for their guides), you might not want to give away any spoilers. IMDb specifically states that you *should* include spoilers, but that might be a relic from an older era of syndicated reruns versus our new era of FOMO[3] binge-watching. I know I wouldn't want to ruin anyone else's catch-up viewing experience of a show or movie everyone else loved that they somehow missed (because they had a toddler, were writing a book, doing their residency or thesis, ensnarled in a lawsuit or divorce, overcoming sickness, providing eldercare, or whatever other "life happened" to cause them to — *GASP!* — miss out on a bit of popular culture). But that's just my $.02.

If you're putting this info into a business-to-business (B2B) portal, something like Cinando.com, MyAFM or MyNATPE, you'll definitely want to show off everything under the hood for distributors and sales agents to facilitate their professional assessments.

This should go without saying (but sadly it can't): *You should never offer commentary on your own content.* You don't get to be both creator and critic. Don't give your opinion of what the general public will think of your material. "*Audiences will love it!*" is unwelcome hyperbole and screams "neophyte."

"And . . . ACTION!"
Write Your Summary

1. Start with your logline.
2. Depending on which version of your logline you're using, make sure it includes, of course *(broken record here but consider this athletic drills or musical scales)*: major character, goal, conflict, setup of your story (catalyst, establish the normal world) and what happens to get it going (inciting incident, escalating stakes).

---

[3] Fear of Missing Out

3. Expand your one-sentence logline into one paragraph highlighting its three-act structure. Think skipping rocks along a lake: just touch, touch, touch out onto the horizon. By default, your first act will get the most attention — about half the word count — with diminishing space (but not drama!) for the subsequent two, implying the accelerating pace.

4. Like the logline (and everything else), your summary is designed to entice the reader to read or the listener to ask to read or view the work you're pitching. Use evocative language that captures the essence of the piece and conjures the world in their mind's eye. . . and intrigues them enough to want more and act on that desire.

Everything is part art, part craft, so do not take this as a formula but rather a rough value sketch:

Sentence #1 = Act I: Setup: Protagonist, Storyworld, Goal, Problem, Action

Sentence #2 = Act I: Protagonist's Plan (Promise of the Premise)

Sentence #3 = Act II: What conflict causes them to change? (Character Arc/Theme)

Sentence #4 = Act III: Climax

Something like that.

For some, it is easier to write the longer synopsis first, then trim down to a summary, like Michelangelo, hacking away at all the marble that doesn't belong in the final sculpture. For others, it's easier for them to build up: logline, summary, synopsis. There is no right or wrong. Whatever works for you.

IMDb lists up to five summaries per title if they present differing viewpoints. Study different summary versions of your comps and see if you can appreciate the distinctions.

Synopsis

A synopsis is a brief description of the work, written in the present tense, detailing what happens in the plot as it unfolds via the narrative structure.

Almost a polished prose version of your beat outline, it's longer and more involved than your summary but not quite yet a full treatment. A synopsis topnotes the antagonist, supporting characters and subplots, love interest, character arc, theme and genre-related obligatory scenes. Whereas the logline shows off your concept, the synopsis gives your writing its first opportunity to shine.

You expanded your logline sentence into a summary paragraph. Your synopsis can now stretch across an entire page. . . up to, say, one and three-quarters of a page. Your two-page "one sheet" must still leave room for your contact info, maybe a logo, usually the logline, and sometimes a title treatment[4] and/or key art, a bio blurb, often with a thumbnail headshot.

COVERAGE VS. MARKETING SYNOPSES

Production companies (and publishing houses) outsource the astonishing volume of submitted material to readers who provide coverage reports to help their bosses decide which projects are actually worth their time to read. Readers are one of the many notorious "gatekeepers" to our industry.

Coverage reports are diagnostic, descriptive documents that facilitate acquisition decisions that vary from agency to fielding entity but they usually include:

• **Project Details**: *Title*, screenwriter, type of material, genre, locale, estimated budget, submitting party
• **Logline** (written by the reader)

---

[4] This is essentially the "logofication" of your title (genre-relevant font and colors).

- **Comments Summary** (paragraph overview of the reader's analysis to come)
- **Plot Synopsis** (1-3 pages, written by the reader)
- **Grade Rubric** (*Excellent, Good, Fair, Poor*) on key elements:
  - Premise
  - Characterization
  - Plot
  - Dialogue
  - Setting
  - Structure
  - Series/Casting Potential (sometimes)
- **Reader's Analysis**
- **Reader's Recommendation** ("PASS," "CONSIDER," or "RECOMMEND")

Some contests provide coverage as part of their entry fee and many writers proactively pay to get coverage of their work to get an honest third-party assessment.[5]

But. . . Can't I Just Use the Coverage Synopsis?

- Students "cheat" using CliffsNotes so they don't have to read the whole book.

- Producers hire readers to provide coverage so they don't have to read all the scripts.

- Your whole goal is to get them to read the script — not facilitate their skipping it.

Coverage provides a synopsis but it's usually done by an exhausted third party trying to get through a stack. Their condensed recitation of the plot allows a creative exec to quickly skim to get a sense of the scope and scale: *are there explosions, stunts, car chases, fight sequences, love scenes?*

---

[5] Script analysis or consultation is different from coverage in that it is far more exhaustive and constructive, targeted to the writer with a goal of improving their script versus vetting it for the industry.

How complicated are they? How many locations? How big is the cast?

Readers can write terrific summaries, synopses and great loglines but their goal is different from yours. They aren't trying to sell your work. They are judging it, often harshly — detailing its strengths and weaknesses — and they are dashing off these analyses as fast as they can. Don't use these to market your work.

That said, coverage can provide an excellent, objective starting place. I always find it fascinating to see what kind of loglines and synopses come back from strangers, how they describe my characters to their bosses or clients. Don't get upset if they are "incorrect." They're overworked. It happens. They are practically transcribing as they read, always on a tight deadline. Not a lot of room left for finesse. But that's not their job. That's your job. And if they didn't get what you intended, perhaps you didn't do your job well enough.

Analogous to "The Customer Is Always Right," "The Reader Is Never Wrong." No one can be wrong about *their experience* of your art. It may change over time or on a second read or viewing, but they are entitled to their reaction. Whether you like it or not.

You may agree or not with their assessment or valuations but their recap is their reduction sauce of what they got out of reading your script — and there's great value in that. If you can get your hands on it (which is rare — but ask for it), coverage can illuminate script problems from an honest, uninvested person's point of view. Yet another fertile opportunity along the write-develop-market-pitch-write continuum. Just as all your comp research illustrated genre obligations and your crosses illuminated breakout collision opportunities, someone else's distillation of what happened — and why — might shine a glaring light on plot holes or credibility or empathy issues. And that's huge.

So, instead of lazily relying on repurposing an unbiased, down and dirty recap of your plot points, bring your mad skills to rewrite it to promote your material. Highlight the cinematic moments. Make them feel the genre, enjoy the plot twists. Engage their senses. Emulate the viewing experience.

Just accelerate the playback speed.

 ## "And . . . ACTION!"
Write Your Synopsis

A good starting place is to take your summary and expand each sentence into a paragraph.

As always, think about your target audience.

If you're pitching an actor to attach as the antagonist or love interest (instead of the protagonist), their tweaked version might amplify that particular role. Every character is the hero of their own movie — even the bad guy and supporting characters.

If you're pitching to a director or a key department head (production designer, stunt coordinator for an action piece, hair/makeup/wardrobe for a period piece, or a monster maker for a horror or sci fi), highlight the creative potential for their medium.

If you're pitching to a geographically devoted equity investor, grant, film commission or prospective joint-venture landlord, play up their beloved setting.

Non-profit? Their issues. It's creative. It's marketing. It's spin. Ad copy is a love letter to your target audience's end game.

One Sheet

One sheets historically referred to movie posters, those 27" × 40" cinema lobby cards. The term still means that to many (especially collectors), but it has morphed into an umbrella term encompassing 8.5" × 11" fliers used at markets to post-cards used at festivals and PDFs emailed all around the world, every day. Pitch fests see every variation along the spectrum, especially from the self-publishing arena.

A one sheet is a bit of a misnomer because it's actually two pages: one *sheet*, printed on both sides. At markets and festivals, these are usually professionally printed, full-color key art and/or production stills on card stock, marketing completed work "in the can." For scripts and concepts in development, they are often just black text on plain white paper — but just as aesthetically laid out (with lots of white space).

One sheets can help you at every stage of the process. Quick skims might glance and review 30% of a one sheet versus 5% of a long pitch deck.

 ## "And . . . ACTION!"
Pull Together Your One Sheet

- *Terrific Title* (in a title treatment if you've got the artistic skills, network or budget)
- Key Art (if you've got any)
- TV Show Format and Length (if relevant)
- Genre
- Best Logline you've ever written
- Intriguing Tagline
- Summary
- Creator's/Rights Owner's Headshot (if you like it) (optional)
- *Brief* credibility-inspiring bio(s) (optional, if there's space — less important than the project)
- Company Logo (optional, if important/relevant)
- **Don't forget your contact info!**

Your one sheet must instantly and effectively communicate everything anyone might need to know to assess if your project fits their mandates, jives with their outlet's brand, aligns with their vision or is a fit for their resources. It must engender sufficient curiosity for them to proactively take the next step.

You never get a second chance to make a first impression.

This single-sheet pitch document should intrigue producers, distributors, actors and directors to make the snap-judgment decision to request the script (or equity investors, the business plan). That's its job. Its only job. It doesn't hang around in files to be referenced later. It creates the impulse or gets tossed. It's not quite junk mail but. . . it has about the same shelf life.

That's a pretty big job for one piece of paper. If it does its job well, it might have to do it over and over again. It should be so self-contained that whomever you pitch to can simply share it with a peer or forward it up the ladder to the Powers That Be, whom they need to convince to get on board. The next best thing to being there, one sheets are the closest you'll get to personally pitching to everyone in the decision-making chain. In this collaborative development relay race, your one sheet is your baton — unifying your passion with clarity — that you must hand off and trust others to carry over every hurdle.

Writers may never need one sheets. Producers use them all the time. But it can make writers stand out from the masses as more professional, especially at pitch fests. But don't confuse "one sheet" to mean all your loglines on one sheet. That says: *"Here's all the inventory I couldn't sell to anyone else. Yard sale!"* Use *one* sheet per project. The *only* exception to this *might* be if you know — *for a fact* — that an independent producer is looking for something really specific, say, a contained-cast, one-location thriller or a Christmas movie of the week. Then — *maybe* — it might be appropriate to put three loglines on one piece of paper with your contact info at the top. But that's because your researched prospect is specifically looking for that yellow needle in a haystack. You're not only offering up several legit possibilities that fit their mandates but you're also presenting yourself as a creative who thrives in that space. If the script you submit is well-executed and gains their confidence but the concept is a miss for one reason or another (they may have a location or star already lined up), your specific proficiency might just shine enough to get you the assignment to polish whosever's script they did buy.

Don't feel like you have to fill the back of the sheet. If your logline, synopsis and contact info feel sufficient on one page, there is art in brevity. Never give them one iota of info that is boring or sub-standard. Don't include a single word that could make them second guess their initial interest. Less is more.

It's a challenge to get the right people in power to read your screenplays. The chasm between a query — or even a successful pitch — to a sale can feel insurmountable. Your one sheet might secure that elusive pitch meeting with legit players or be an excellent leave-behind to help you cinch a script request after a wobbly pitch. Stay focused on your goal: Get them to read the script. And always be networking.

Query Letters

Queries are short feeler notes, usually via email. A little more than your logline, but a lot less than your one sheet, queries are essentially crisp cover letters that don't actually "cover" anything (yet).

Journalists query magazine editors. Authors query publishers. Writers query agents and managers. But because Hollywood is so litigious and inundated with armies of gatekeepers blockading the tsunami of unsolicited materials, unrepped screenwriters and content creators must often query production and distribution companies just to request permission to pitch. Along the lines of the childhood game *"Mother May I?"* queries ask for the greenlight to *"take one step forward"* and follow up with their script or film or schedule a phone or office-pitch appointment.

Unfortunately, many queries rarely reach their intended recipient. Or, if they do, they are bulk dismissed sight unseen by their systems as SPAM or deleted unread as junk mail, rarely securing the coveted approval. Sadly, the low-hanging fruit you can secure affirmative responses from are often the entities on the periphery of the business that make up the bulk of the horror stories. But sometimes your access alternatives are slim pickings. Or you're using a virtual platform or filling out an online form. Or, you're reaching out creatively to people outside the business to garner all different kinds of support.

If you must query cold, do your best to network to find any mutual acquaintances who might be game to initiate a third-party–endorsing introduction. Or at least let you use their name. A lukewarm acquaintance-of-an-acquaintance approach beats out-of-the-blue from a random stranger.

"And . . . ACTION!"
Draft Your Customizable
Master Query Letter

Your subject line is as important a trigger as a clickbait headline. If they don't open the email, all this effort is for naught. If you met the prospect at an event, or heard them speak or read an article they wrote or were quoted in, these can at least serve as point-of-reference runway lights. Ideally make it relevant to them.

Prospects off your comps list provide built-in ice breakers. Authentically praise them for their work, point out a specific connection between their relevant credit and your project, then pivot to yours. Easy breezy.

If you have no connection whatsoever, go for establishing your own credibility as a writer, highlighting any prominent writing awards you've won. If you've got nothing, you're back to relying on the strength of the concept.

Start off with some attention-grabbing hook, any connection you may have, your *brief* credentials. Give the title, genre/format and logline and close with a specific request: May you send the script or schedule a pitch meeting (or even just a quick call).

Don't attach anything to your query. So few professionals accept random submissions to begin with, they will be leery of unsolicited scripts being emailed without a signed release. Or worse, inadvertently downloading a virus from a stranger. Attachments will likely be stripped or cause your missive to be deleted unopened. Keep everything in the body of the email.

Don't just paste your one sheet into the email: That's too much for an initial contact. Trim and customize. A query shouldn't be more than a few sentences to a couple paragraphs at the most. And don't offer the one sheet or pitch package (unless that's all you've got on the project). You want them to read the script. Or let you pitch. Don't put an unnecessary hurdle between where you're at and where you want to be. That's just an easy, intermediary excuse to say "No." If *they ask* for that, of course, provide it. That's an understandable baby step on their part. But *you* ask — directly — for what *you* want: two steps forward.

Why Them? Why You? Why Now?

Why are you reaching out *to them*? Specifically? Mass email blasts are like burst-bazookaing wet balls of toilet paper against a ceiling to see what will stick. Not much will and. . . would you really want those that do? Target. Be specific. Be relevant. Have a reason. Use their mission statement back to them. Rephrase their brand to describe your content. If it doesn't fit, you might not be querying the right entity.

Why are you the perfect scribe to have originated this project? What in your backstory perfectly poised you to bring this story to light? Own it. Share why your unique worldview and sensibility gives this telling of the story authenticity.

And why now? What makes the timing of this project ideal for them to bring it to market? Does it tap into the Zeitgeist of what's going on in the culture today? If that's not obvious, frame it for them. Show them their point of entry, and how it might be more relevant to their target audience than they realize. Something they might have missed — or been looking for.

BASIC DEVELOPMENT & MARKETING MATERIALS

Beat Outline

A beat outline is a matter-of-fact, scene-by-scene breakdown of what happens (or will happen) in a script. Beat sheets can literally be just bullet lists of plot and turning points, detailing the chronological or story order of events; a diagram tracking the character's arc across the scenes or a few pages of prose. An at-a-glance skeletal treatment, usually without dialogue, beat outlines highlight the otherwise invisible structure and where key exposition is planted. Rarely used as marketing deliverables, beat outlines can be useful ideation tools for solitary writers as well as great course-correcting diagnostic development tools for collaborative teams.

There are as many approaches to writing a beat outline as there are to writing a script. You could follow Chris Vogler's adaptation of Joseph Campbell's seminal Hero's Journey work applied specifically to screenplays; Michael Hauge's great commercial Hollywood approach; Billy Mernit's seven beats from his *Writing the Romantic Comedy*; Blake Snyder's revolutionary *Save the Cat!* approach. . . to name just a few of the major players.

BILLY MERNIT'S SEVEN *WRITING THE ROMANTIC COMEDY* BEATS

1. Setup = The Chemical Equation
2. Catalyst = The Cute Meet (aka "Meet Cute")
3. 1st Turning Point = A Sexy Complication
4. Midpoint = The Hook
5. 2nd Turning Point = The Swivel
6. Crisis/Climax = The Dark Moment
7. Resolution = Joyful Defeat

Whether you opt to 3" × 5" card, whiteboard, spreadsheet, Morning Page scribble or use one of the many software programs, almost all of these processes result in some sort of an ordered list of escalating stakes in a three-act structure. Delineate a clear line of action for your protagonist. The second turning point (the event that occurs at the second-act curtain) triggers the climax. The pace of the third act should build to a crescendo. It can be valuable to keep this bullet list nearby for quick reference and modifications. This can also be instrumental for development meetings. But it's rarely a marketing tool.

 GAME SHOW BEAT OUTLINES

Beat outlines can highlight a game show's concept and effectively tease the inner workings of its architecture. If it's a simple show, use a beat outline. Just simple headlines. Walk through no more than four of five sets of key beats.

Treatment

A treatment is a detailed, present-tense narration of all the characters and major "beats" or moments of the story. Almost a short story expansion of the synopsis, treatments can be virtually any length from a couple pages to a couple hundred, though most range between 5–35 pages.

Not all spec writers bother with treatments, but they can serve as terrific road maps for project discovery. They can serve lone writers as a diagnostic tool to illuminate story problems by distilling narrative action lines. They can also be used to sell speculative story ideas into paid assignments to execute. Usually breaking down books, feature or pilot scripts, treatments are also incredibly instrumental as a collaborative development communication device.

TREATMENTS

I had a teacher once, in UCLA's screenwriting certificate program, who for *three months* wouldn't let a single one of us type "Fade In" (i.e., start our scripts) — and we were in a screen*writing* class! It was annoying. It drove us all crazy. We spent the entire course hammering out every last bit of minutia (you know: "minor" stuff like character arcs, subplots, theme, etc.) for our treatments.

My first project, *The Courage to Love,* a $5.5-million-dollar Lifetime Original Movie that starred Vanessa Williams, was set up based on the strength of the treatment I had just learned how to master in his class. I now consider Frank McAdams not only one of the best teachers I ever had, but I consider myself lucky enough to call him my friend.

Scott Frank admitted his treatments were even longer than Elmore Leonard's books (*Out of Sight, Get Shorty*) he adapted! But that's his process. And he's been incredibly successful.

There is no right or wrong — there is just your creative process. Whatever that may be. And that will likely evolve over time. As your expertise increases, you may hone different approaches. Your strategies may vary based on genre or the source of the idea. Other collaborators' personalities, communication styles or work methods may need to be accommodated. As Tim Gunn of *Project Runway* always says: "Make it work."

There are several different types of treatments and they have varied purposes. Some writers write beat outlines, brainstorming several different ideas, then full treatments to explore only the most promising to decide which premise has the most potential to warrant typing "Fade In." This is often what development with a studio or director might look like with a hired writer. Steps and phases allowing all the players in the collaborative process to chime in at each stage. The hiring entity may even have commissioned multiple simultaneous treatments to solicit different takes from a cross-section of writers. As these are usually "write for hire" assignments, the producers are then free to cherry pick the elements they like of each and hire one writer to integrate these selections. Producers may use this treatment to package the project even before commissioning the actual script.

Other writers write the first draft of their screenplay in a flash of inspiration, then come back and reverse engineer its outline and treatment afterwards to sort out any derailments. Often, this final document is ultimately polished into a spec selling treatment.

CHARACTER BREAKDOWNS VS. CASTING BREAKDOWNS

Character Breakdowns vary from writer to educational program and work experience, but often they entail profiles of backstory that may or may not ever make it into the script that the writer — and sometimes even the actor — will develop. Interestingly, Aaron Sorkin said in his Masterclass that he never develops these because if it isn't seen on camera, if it isn't shot, it doesn't exist. You may want to only include that which is actually detailed in the script, describing your character and their actions.

Casting Breakdowns are the brief descriptions sent to casting agents and breakdown services when the project is auditioning actors for the roles. These might follow a format looking something like this:

CHARACTER FIRST NAME LAST NAME (Age as a # or range), race (only if relevant to the story, otherwise write/cast color-blind). First impression characteristic, 2–4 precise adjectives that sharply define the divergent angles of the character's persona. The mask he/she projects to the world as well as his or her authentic interior life. Flaws, character quirks and idiosyncrasies. *What does he or she want? Fear? Get?* Brief phrases about relationship interactions and plot action.

While extras and insignificant under–five-line speaking roles might have placeholder names like "Ugly Goon" for the convenience of development, it's a courtesy to the dignity of the auditioning actors that when you shift from a selling script to a shooting script, or at least break out sides (the few pages of a scene the actors will audition with), that you give these roles character names.

Treatments can be an invaluable development and marketing tool. Not only can they help improve the literary property and serve as a marketing deliverable, they help prepare you to pitch. There might be myriad variations more than I have listed here but what follows are the generally accepted umbrella categories.

Development Treatments

Development treatments aren't normally marketing tools. They can be polished to serve that purpose but usually they are diagnostic, often transcriptive. Sometimes functioning almost as development meeting minutes, they can track everyone's agreed-upon input and the direction for the project, making sure everyone's on the same page, writing and making the same movie. It's easier to recognize a verbal misunderstanding of a lengthy discussion when it's spelled out in black and white. Correcting a sentence or paragraph on the page is much easier than fixing a scene or entire performance if a character goes off the rails of intention.

Writing treatments can give writers an objective, 10,000-foot bird's-view of their script. It's easy to get lost in the weeds. If you find yourself spackling plot holes, glossing over credibility issues or trying to bury obvious pace problems with scenes that don't turn the narrative, are predictable or — *GASP!* — boring, writing a treatment might really accelerate your rewrite efforts.

Distilling the idea down to treatment form might reveal that, no matter how brilliantly you execute, the concept itself might be a slog to market. Doesn't mean don't pursue, but this epiphany should give you pause to consider how invested you are in the idea — and how much work you have ahead of you — or maybe how to heighten the concept at the skeletal stage.

Marketing Treatments

Marketing treatments are written specifically to sell. Your treatment should highlight the major turning points of each act and, scene by scene, the significant value changes and reversals but still have all the color, flavor and drama of the finished piece. Treatments range in length all over the place: seven to twenty pages is reasonable.

It's likely that instead of a marketing treatment, you (or your producer) would use a pitch package (with a synopsis); but your prospect may specifically request a treatment. To some, the terminology may overlap, their distinctions irrelevant. Regardless, here are two ends of the spectrum of the elements you'd want to polish and have market-ready.

Minimalistic Treatment

1. Cover Page
   a. Title
   b. Writer's/Rights Holder's Name and Contact Info
   c. Logline
   d. Plot Summary
2. Extended Synopsis (2–10 pages)
   a. Act I (1–3 paragraphs)

     i. Setup and/or Catalyst

     ii. Inciting Incident

     iii. 1st Turning Point (Plot Point I)

   b. Act II Mid-Point (2–6 paragraphs)

   c. Act III (1–3 paragraphs)

     i. 2nd Turning Point

     ii. Climax

     iii. Denouement

3. Character List (1–2 pages)

   a. One page of thumbnail character sketches (ages, leadoff characteristics, vocations, relationships, etc.)

DON'T PUT YOUR © # ON YOUR TITLE PAGE

While you should register the first expression of each idea with the Writers Guild of America and copyright your screenplays, it is not recommended you put either number on any of your literary assets while marketing. It's a bit like adding your driver's license or Social Security number. We get it. You've got one. It's assumed your intellectual property (literary asset: script, book, etc.) is registered. That's what a professional would do. If you get a deal, they'll ask for these numbers soon enough.

Extended Treatment

1. Cover Page

   a. Title

   b. Writer's/Rights Holder's Name and Contact Info

   c. Logline

2. Character Breakdowns

  a. This could be:

    i. full-blown character profiles (backstories) for each main character and a paragraph for minor characters

    ii. classic casting breakdowns

    iii. placed at the end as a reference instead of at the front

3. Plot

  a. Act I: Set the scene, dramatize the main conflicts

  b. Act II: How do the conflicts introduced in Act I lead to a crisis?

  c. Act III: Dramatize the final conflict and resolution

Movie of the Week 7-Act Structure

While streaming outlets are changing this model, broadcast movies of the week have traditionally followed a seven-act structure, allowing for mini-cliffhangers at every commercial (act) break, the biggest one being at the hour break (the greatest risk window of losing audience members to another show). Act I is usually about 20 minutes with the first scene establishing the protagonist and her world, the second being the inciting incident. The rest of the acts average about 12 minutes of six scenes, escalating in pace 'til the climax and resolution.

Game Show Treatments

Six pages. The first two pages set up the idea. The remaining four offer a brief outline of what a typical episode contains (e.g., five rounds of a straightforward sports quiz) and the mechanics of the show. Bring your love of the subject matter to life on paper through examples that sing. Treatments that are too dry don't work. Provide fun — but brief — examples of the types of trivia questions or obstacles.

Documentary Treatments

Documentaries are part journalism, part filmmaking — all storytelling. Documentarians never know what they're gonna get. It is uncontrolled cinema, with the only semblance of control coming from the edit bay. Writing treatments for documentaries can be challenging as they are works-in-progress almost 'til their premiere. Thus, you might be outlining what no one could possibly predict.

 REALITY TV DOCUMENTARY EXAMPLE

Accused murderer and New York real estate heir Robert Durst reached out to filmmaker Andrew Jarecki, volunteering to be interviewed. While talking to himself in the bathroom mirror *during shooting*, oblivious that his mic was still on, Durst admitted: *"What the hell did I do? Killed them all, of course."* But no one realized they had this incriminating gem in the footage 'til well into the trial. But the day before the finale aired, he was arrested on first-degree murder charges. The six-episode limited series *Jinx* (HBO, 2015) went on to win two Emmys, a Peabody and a PGA award.

Like any other content, the "big idea" is what will help sell or promote documentary projects. There has to be a unifying theme and an identified target audience. If you have finished the project, you'll have a polished premise elaborating the outcome. If not, your working logline can simply present the central character, world or issue you intend to explore. If you are pitching for a production grant, you might not know what you'll get in the can. Of course, those funding documentaries appreciate this. If you're pitching for distribution or post support, you might not yet have discovered your story amongst all the raw footage organized in your bins. Your narrative position will likely influence distribution decisions (save for the most agnostic streaming networks) but you can detail your inspirations, intentions and expectations.

What makes your approach evocative? What are the struggles? What (or who) are the obstacles and threats? How will you cinematically dramatize these issues? What uniquely qualifies you (or your on-screen host or other members of your team) to tell this story?

The body of the synopsis can detail the images and sounds that (will) dramatize the beginning, middle and end. Identify the known areas of conflict and projected opportunities for drama. You can describe the completed (or proposed) interview subjects, locations and topics discussed or questions planned.

Treatment Tips

As with everything else you use to market your literary assets, the writing has to be excellent. Compelling. Emulating the mood, pace and tone of your story. The narrative should always (for every deliverable) be in the present tense. Even if it's a flashback or nonlinear structure, everything we see unfolds before our eyes as if it's happening right now — because, for the audience, it is.

Don't use technical language, jargon or camera angles (unless you're a writer/director refining an internal scriptment to shoot). Don't ALL CAP sound effects, it's distracting. Just tell us the story and conjure it vividly in our mind's eye.

As in a screenplay, you get only what we can see or hear — but don't write "we see" or "we hear" — just tell us what happens. Let us get lost in the telling. Save your character's interior thoughts for your novelization. Only write what we can actually shoot.

As in your script, ALL CAP each character's name the first time they appear in the treatment. This signifies to the reader that this is a new character. It also speeds their scrolling-back search if they forget who's who. Future references can be whatever you consistently call the character in Title Case. Use last names if you want to signify familial relationships. Use honorifics (Dr., Sergeant, Reverend) if pertinent to the story.

Put their age as a numeral in brackets right after their name. Don't make us dig. You could use a decade, too (20s). Give a brief but specific description of the character's persona — not their physical description unless it is critical to the plot (e.g., "one-armed albino").

Use clear time and space transitions ("At school the next day,"), mini slugs (partial sluglines without the INT./EXT. or DAY/NIGHT). If you think it'll ease the read, break out and bold headings with act breaks. If TV, call out the tag and tease. Typically, treatments don't include dialogue (scriptments do).

Scriptment

Just as the name implies, a scriptment (script + treatment) is a hybrid that combines the elements of both. Scriptments were inadvertently made famous by James Cameron when his 1994 scriptment for *Avatar* was leaked during pre-production almost fifteen years later. John Hughes, Zak Penn, Mark Duplass and others have been known to write scriptments as well. Like some book-adaptation treatments, scriptments can be as long as or even longer than scripts. Cameron's *Titanic* (1997) scriptment was 131 pages long. Sometimes the screenplay format is circumvented altogether by shooting directly off the scriptment.

Largely favored by writer/directors, scriptments are often integrated with storyboards. They may or may not use sluglines (and their use may be inconsistent). Scriptments do heavy development and pre-production lifting rather than functioning as typical sales or marketing pieces.

While they may seem like an unnecessary step between a treatment and a full-blown script, scriptments can — counter-intuitively — actually streamline the process. They provide a development shorthand to facilitate speedily beating out key plot points that must be hit, in which scenes, and placehold pivotal dialogue (formatted in the center, just like in a screenplay).

They are not common. They are not for everyone. None of these literary efforts are. Pick and choose what works for you, this project and the current team's process.

Script

Nothing is more important than the script (or the protectable, high-concept TV format).

Period.

Full stop.

Let me reiterate: *Nothing is more important than the script.*

We could end this section right there.

There is so much more to say on this topic that we couldn't even begin to skim the surface. Bookstores, the internet and cottage industries of workshops, conferences and webinars are full of advice on every angle and element of screenwriting — but this is not a book on screenwriting, a precious and noble art form.

Everything starts and ends with great writing — or at least a marketable, high-concept idea that is ultimately developed into great content. The script has to be brilliant. Your distinctive voice and crisp, elegant style must portray fascinating characters with unique worldviews in unpredictable situations and interesting milieus that delight, surprise and, most of all, *move* your readers.

A whole house of cards will be built on this tiny little stack of paper. You will invest *years* of your life. Your best creative energies — all your professional relationships and resources — will get sucked into the vortex that is this black hole. Make sure it's worth it.

It all comes back to the quality of what you're selling. You owe it to yourself to ensure that your screenplay (or whatever literary material it is that you're hawking) is solid enough to warrant all the effort it will catalyze and urgently and relentlessly demand from every aspect of your life.

A fantastic script can open up worlds of opportunities beyond itself.

Selling vs. Shooting Scripts

You may see scripts online that have scene numbers in the margins or even camera shots. Those are shooting scripts, intended for production, not literary sales. Your goal is to write a selling script. The technical stuff can bog down the enjoyment of a brisk and easy read with premature, possibly even erroneous detail. That can all be added later by the appropriate parties (even if it's you). Right now? To sell? Streamline the read.

The industry rule of thumb is that on-screen minutes = script pages. Shorter is almost always better as there is the perception that every page/minute impacts the budget (or broadcast commercial time). Comedy dialogue and action can take more space on the page than the pace of their execution. Sometimes the shorter the script, the less accurate this gauge can be, but it's a generally accepted rule.

INDUSTRY SCRIPT-LENGTH BALLPARK

Feature Film Screenplay	89–120 pages
Hour-Long TV Script	45–60 pages
Half-Hour TV Script	25–45 pages

Most professional scripts right now average between 95–107 pages. Thrillers and comedies tend to be at the shorter end of the spectrum (89–105). Sustaining the tension of the lie, joke, mystery or suspense is self-limiting. Book and true-life story adaptations can often run at the longer end of the spectrum as well as period pieces and sci fi because they usually need more words to depict new or less familiar worlds.

PROTECT YOUR INTELLECTUAL PROPERTY

You can't copyright an idea — only its execution.

Copyright is almost always your strongest legal position. To best protect your material at the earliest possible point you can evidence ownership, copyright your first draft of a script or manuscript (or even the synopsis or treatment).

Electronic Copyright: *https://eco.copyright.gov*

You can register your scripts with the Writers Guild of America even if you're not a member of the union. To date-stamp early-stage film and television ideas, you could register your outline, synopsis, treatment, pitch deck, proposal, stage play, novel, short story — you get the idea. Virtually any literary asset could be submitted to the WGA, as a reputable third party, to hold and — should they officially be called upon to do so — to document proof of authorship claims.

Writers Guild of America Registration

West: *https://www.wgawregistry.org/registration.asp*

East: *https://www.wgaeast.org/script_registration?rm=material_form*

TIP: *How might you copyright an unscripted program?* As copyright protects the expression of the idea, you could document — in written form — how your unscripted reality show format might play out by drafting a hypothetical pilot or sample episode with "avatar" or archetype contestants, hosts or personalities.

ADVANCED MARKETING & DEVELOPMENT
═══ DELIVERABLES ═══

Pitch Package

A pitch package is an amalgamation of the materials you have assembled as your most succinct, polished expression of the content captured on the page or screen. The CliffsNotes brochure of your entire project. The pitch on the page.

A catchall, generic term that can mean different things to different professionals, a pitch package may reference anything from one sheets to investor pitch decks, series bibles to distributor proposals, brand presentations for product placement to look books to attach talent. A pitch *package* may actually refer to an entire collection of documents, such as the one sheet, pilot script and series bible or even the feature screenplay, budget, schedule and business plan. Often with supporting images, sometimes with multimedia elements such as an embedded sizzle reel, trailer, rip-o-matic or external links, they are the guts of what make up many business plans and websites.

As creatively and tonally meticulous as loglines, but encompassing the structure, themes and visuals of the screenplay or format, pitch packages condense all your conceptual material into engaging ad copy that encapsulates the entire scope of your project from your title, genre and logline to characters, themes and storytelling structure. Not only detailing your protagonist or host and their world and journey, these proposals also profile the credibility of the team behind the strategies employed and their proposed execution. Coming from a writer, the focus may be purely creative whereas a producer might build on all that to add practical physical production elements, financing, distribution and marketing strategies.

Depending on who you're pitching to — or where you are in the process — pitch packages can be right-brain creative, left-brain financial, or industry savvy. . . or often a combination of all three. Often tweaked as the project evolves and customized to fit each prospect's mandates.

An Excellent Answer to
"What else have you got on this. . .?"

Nothing beats a face-to-face pitch, but we work in a visual, collaborative industry — often virtually and nonlinearly, around the globe and across timelines, meandering up through vertically integrated conglomerates across a puzzle of affinity partners. Flawlessly executed, pitch packages can follow a query to secure you that elusive pitch meeting or serve as a brilliant leave-behind. Even better, they can be a customized follow-up clincher, integrating new insights and prospect-specific information gleaned during the pitch.

These marketing materials, exclusively for internal, business-to-business presentations, empower every player to pitch up and around the decision-making chain with unified integrity. Marketable pitch packages can preserve the integrity of your pitch and exude your passion in your absence. They can be a game changer for your career.

Pitch Package Elements

Right back to Journalism 101. Top note the most important elements: the Who, What, Where, When, Why — and sometimes How:

The 5 Ws

WHAT is it you're pitching?

WHEN and WHERE might it air?

WHO are you pitching?

WHO is it about?

WHO is it right for?

      ~ Target Audience?

      ~ TV Channel?

WHY is it right for whomever you're pitching to?

WHY is it right for right now?

HOW are you going to tell the story?

    ... or pull off the physical production?

    ... or find your audience?

Plain and simple. Of course, more readily described than accomplished. Pitch packages are an art form in and of themselves. Like the nightly news, intrigue your audience with the most important information. Don't bury your lead or your punch line. Your pitch package should creatively address:

- If it's a feature, start with the genre.
- If it's a TV series, define the format.
  - *Is it half-hour or hour-long?*
  - *Single camera? Multi-camera?*
  - *Scripted or unscripted?*
    - If it's scripted:
      - *Is it comedy or drama? Or dramedy?*
      - *Sitcom or procedural?*
      - *Serial or episodic?*
    - If it's unscripted:
      - *Is it structured or unstructured?*
      - *Docudrama? Structured docusoap? Cinéma vérité? Infotainment?*
      - *Amateur talent show? Social experiment?*
      - *True crime? Court show? Legal documentary?*
  - *How many episodes to a season?*
    - *Broadcast 22?*
    - *10-episode limited event series?*
- *Where and how might it be programmed on television? At a festival?*
  - *Would it be perfect for a midnight festival screening?*
- *Is it appropriate for a four-quadrant, mainstream broadcast network audience?*

Four Major Audience Quadrants

Males Over 25	Females Over 25
Males Under 25	Females Under 25

- *Is it ready for prime time?*
  - ○ *Is it edgier, better suited for late night? Or cable?*
  - ○ *Destined for an over-the-top TV streaming outlet like Netflix, Amazon or Hulu?*
- *If it's kids' programming, should it be slotted for morning, afternoon or bedtime?*
- *Is there a specific gender, ethnicity, socioeconomic or psychographic[1] demographic that it targets?*
- *Is there any live or social media audience interaction?*

Pitch Package Construction

Cover Page

Key art, title treatment (omit cover page if you don't have key art)

Possibly: tagline, contact info, company logo

Condensed pitch packages might even include the genre, subgenre (if applicable), possibly even the logline

Overview

All the info from above that didn't go on the "cover": title, genre/subgenre and/or TV format, logline, tagline, target audience (MPAA rating if relevant), (the guts of your one sheet, less compressed)

Possibly even a paragraph summary here (instead of or to complement the logline)

---

[1] Qualitative attributes include: personality, values, opinions, attitudes, interests and lifestyles (sometimes referred to as AIO variables: Activities, Interests and Opinions)

Story Summary/Synopsis

This could be a paragraph to even five pages. One to one-and-a-half pages is a good standard.

Main Characters

Just the key characters. This could be just your protagonist and antagonist, only your two romantic leads, your ensemble of main characters, the reality host or celeb family — whatever is appropriate for your project.

You might want to add any minor, actor bait roles — any "And. . ." or "With. . ." stunt-casting opportunities; obviously, especially when submitting to secure those attachments.

Images

Many pitch packages are purely text. If you're a writer, that is all that is expected. Feel free to go back to writing. Lucky you!

If you're a producer (or trying to get other professionals to reconsider you in that light), you'll be well served to populate your pitch package with good production-value visuals to the maximum of your resources.

Bios

Professional headshots and bios of writer(s), creators, producers and most-relevant team members and/or department heads.

If you have a high-profile, officially attached TV show-runner or feature director, she will likely lead off this section as it should be ordered according to the weight each party brings to the project — and they will "helm." Yes, painfully, this may leave you, the true originator, at the bottom. It sucks. I know. *Trust me: I know!* But this is not a legal document ranking ownership or contribution thus far: It's marketing. *What will immediately instill confidence in your prospect? What will appease fears and worries? What will get you — and your project — to the next step?* Keep your eye on the ball.

If your bio needs to be beefed up: *Has your writing been produced? Won any awards? What relevant life experience or subject matter expertise has uniquely earned you the right to tell this story? Can you make that relevant to the genre?*

IMDb allows 2,550 words for a bio. That's great for search-engine-optimization but you should shoot for 1/20th that for your pitch package.

Contact Info

You'd be amazed how many people forget to add this! I'm not kidding. Over and over again. Shocking. Your contact info (or whomever you want fielding responses) should be on everything!

If you have a production company, you might want to add your company logo. Alternately, this could go in the footer or as a watermark. Don't feel the need to appear "bigger" by putting your (other industry) company's business logo. This could backfire in many ways. Just put what's relevant to this project. Even if you have a company, you may still just submit as an individual, especially if you're a writer, with no plans to produce yourself.

If you have an entertainment attorney or even an agent or manager who's "hip pocketing" you (meaning they haven't officially taken you on as a client and they are merely doing you a favor by submitting the project on your behalf), you probably want to list *your* contact info rather than theirs. No one will respond quicker or with more passion than you. They may slip your project in a company envelope or slap their branded cover on it — or they might even replace your contact info with theirs (or ask you to provide it that way). Just be sure that if any of your submissions generate any heat, your prospect will be greeted by a responsive project champion.

Style/Format

If you are working with a production company, a packaging agent or manager, some entities have strict templates that unify their pitch packages, PowerPoint decks and reels in terms of logos, colors, structure and sequencing. I did development for a production company affiliated with a hedge fund that required all of us to have unified headshots against the same backdrop (original fine art of the company's owner). If you're affiliated in such a way as to be subject to someone else's style guide, then, of course, honor that. If not, consider branding your own design.

Pitch Deck

A pitch "deck" often refers to a pitch package delivered as a PowerPoint, Keynote, Google Slides or other presentation software — or even as a website — instead of via word processing software (such as MS Word, Pages or Google Docs). The metaphor implying that the slides or web pages are stacked like a deck of playing cards. Pitch decks can be saved as PDFs and emailed or printed, so as to be almost identical in delivery to a traditional pitch package.

The primary difference is that pitch decks tend to be very image-oriented, almost like a look book, with one thought or point per slide. The obvious upside to pitch decks is that they are very visual. A prospect can literally "flip" quickly through to get the gist of the top notes of a project. They can serve as a terrific invisible teleprompt for verbal pitches with the images maintaining visual structure stimulus. Color-coding backgrounds (by acts, green for money/financials — whatever), can serve as a subliminal ticking clock cues.

On the flip side of its benefits are its drawbacks. Pitch decks are not conducive to lots of text. This format does not lend itself to character breakdowns, vision statements, bios, spreadsheets for budgets or investor waterfalls or schedules.

 Hot Tip! Use 96-point font for headlines, 14-point font for details

Look Books, Mood Boards & EPKs

A look book or a mood board is a collection of evocative reference photos and/or illustrations that paint a picture of the intended visual style.

Likened to the project's coffee-table book, look books used to be the exclusive domain of directors, pitching themselves to producers to illustrate their vision, how they'd approach the cinematics in order to secure the assignment. Once tapped, the director often becomes the recipient of department heads' look books, pitching their unique takes of the elements within their expertise, trying to nail their own gigs or vision.

Producers raising private equity might use look books to demonstrate the range of their short-listed directors' styles and prospective actors' headshots. Production stills from "in-the-can" productions accommodate press releases to beautify electronic press kits (EPKs). Writers have been known to use their own variations at home as vision board inspiration or to keep them on track with keywords and themes, or actor goals.

In "the old days" (pre-internet and home color printers), look books could be anything from professionally printed exclusive runs of full-color glossy brochures to magazine cut-outs glued to poster board. Today, it's so easy to beautifully and affordably print one-offs at home or bind them professionally at consumer retail chains. So much is communicated via email and online platforms, these documents may never even be printed at all. All this internal development may simply populate the project's website, Facebook page or group, or Pinterest board.

Once in pre-production, department heads, especially cinematographers, production designers, art directors, location scouts, transportation heads, costume designers, even the hair and makeup glam squad may use their version of a look book to communicate their vision to the director to ensure they are capturing shared sensibilities through their artistic media, be it practical location and vehicle options, lighting and color scheme ideas; character development as expressed through wardrobe, hair and makeup (time-tracking through scars and bruises or the evolution or disintegration of a character's "look") or even via the language of weapons and stunts. These can be terrific, collaborative reference tools, posted on the walls of the production office, to help keep everyone on the same page from development through soft prep all the way through principal photography. Everyone in this collaborative art form has different means of expressing their contribution and look books can be a way of seeing every facet come together.

Some writers, directors or department heads will create separate mood boards for each character. Wardrobe designers making period pieces might have a dedicated costumes page. Photo-driven platforms like Facebook albums, Pinterest boards, Instagram or Flickr can be useful. You could even create separate, secret Pinterest boards for each department or project in development. As the images are culled and refined and the project moves into pre-production or marketing, a curated set could slowly populate a public Pinterest board to generate consistent daily engagement — and enhanced discovery and shareability — showing how that vision was manifested through principal photography production stills. This could be used as bonus material for crowdfunders, as a series before the premiere or to ramp up for local screenings event marketing.

But most importantly, these assets support catchers who must turn around and pitch your project up the ladder without you present.

Just as you pick and choose each word for your script, pitch, and the ad copy of your marketing materials, be extremely selective with your photos. Don't be the first-time grandparent sharing "just a few" (hundred) pics of the new baby (who's now going off to college). Skip rocks. . . just a touch, here and there. Significant moments. Arresting images that each reveal a thousand words, framing context. And not a one that is off point.

Images can range from your project's key art, comps' posters, character images (screen grabs of actors in similar roles), cast headshots (if they are attached or capture the feeling or stature of the type of actor you envision), wardrobe or accessory pictures, screen grabs of locations, stunts, vehicles, world. Pepper your pitch package with images that evoke your vision. A documentary might start with a profound image of the problem explored. A factual television format might collage images of the crime scene or court case. A fictional feature might capture the essence of the milieu or Zeitgeist through imagery.

There are dozens of royalty-free, online photo sources. Provided your pitch materials are only used in business-to-business pitch meetings, they can contain virtually anything that helps you communicate your vision.

FREE PHOTO RESOURCES

- Unsplash.com
- Shutterstock.com
- Pixabay.com
- Pexels.com
- Gratisography.com

Another great resource for location images are film commissions' websites. Most have keyword-searchable galleries. Check out the California Film Commission's CinemaScout at *ca.reel-scout.com*. You don't have to have these locations secured if you're just giving a sense of the world as backdrop for your presentations.

If you are contemplating shooting in whatever city or state offers the best tax incentives or where the production funds might come from, you might consider creating slightly different iterations of the same look book or pitch deck, just varying the photos to highlight iconic images of wherever you're going to shoot or photos that are representative of all of your possible locales.

Every concept should be unique so that it requires customized marketing materials. Different shows dictate different pitch styles and assets that best reflect what's being pitched. The key is to keep everything organic to the concept, character and world.

Let's say, for example, you have a sophisticated, high-octane, pulpy, one-hour action drama. The visual execution of your look book should capture that and be less about generic, gratuitous action sequences any stunt coordinator could competently conjure and more about highlighting what's organic to defining your specific character in his or her milieu.

TV Series Bible

A bible is essentially the treatment for your proposed series, illustrating in a compelling way what brings the story to the door week after week. Whereas feature treatments show how a script wraps up its story in under two hours, a TV series marketing bible demonstrates how a handful to a hundred episodes are launched via the pilot.

Bibles serve multiple purposes crisscrossing the development-marketing continuum. A one sheet could be expanded into a five-page marketing bible, whose sole goal is to get a person in power to read the pilot. The minutia of seasons of a show could be tracked through one hundred pages or more of a full-blown writers' room repository. Or even a document provided to instruct future writers or advise episode directors how the show's outlook should be manifested in each storyline.

Whether as actual pitch deliverables or simply as advance preparatory workouts for high stakes verbal presentations, creating a show bible not only improves your script, it empowers your pitch.

Marketing vs. Development vs. Writers' Room Bibles

 SCRIPTED BIBLES SPECTRUM[2]

New Girl's pitch bible was a successful, breezy eight pages, which included some bulleted beat lists.

Grey's Anatomy bible, that Shonda Rhimes shared in her Masterclass, is 19 pages of pure brilliance including a snippet of dialogue and theme for each of the first 12 episodes with convenient bulleted lists.

Stranger Things' marketing bible for the eight-hour sci-fi horror epic is 22 pages, but it's really less than 11 pages of text. Every other page is a full-page, tonally specific image, so it's really half look book.

---

[2] I keep a library of samples for educational purposes. If you are looking for something in particular, email me at *Author@HeatherHale.com* and I'll share it if I have it — or try to help you track it down.

Terra Nova had a separate eleven-page document detailing the arcs and mythology, characters' secrets and plans, the families, incidents and arcs as well as how they scripted the dinosaurs on a realistic TV-scale schedule and budget.

Star Trek Voyager's bible's 39 pages cover backstory, one page per continuing characters' background, a press release, production information, character descriptions, a glossary of terms, actor and creator bios. They also had a separate 37-page technical primer that helped writers know everything from which button to push to fire the phasers to emergency procedures to a celestial bestiary.

Stargate SG-1 Season 3's writer's bible was 121 pages.

Scripted Marketing Bible

A pilot script can't get sold without a series bible, but a series bible could get sold without a pilot script. If your bible shows off your ability to express your compelling idea, you could get hired to write the pilot you have proposed (instead of writing it on spec).

What's the Story Engine?

A story engine is the reliable, structural mechanism that ensures your show won't run out of episode ideas. It's the design element that promises endless storytelling possibilities.

It gives commissioners confidence in your show's longevity — suggesting your show might have the staying power to make it to the traditional, celebratory 100-episode syndication mark, or even just through a limited run. It frees writers' rooms to explore the full spectrum of potential topics and scenarios while staying organically unified with the show's vision. It keeps audiences intrigued through commercial breaks, across weeks and over hiatuses.

Story engines are a pivotal difference between film and television. Feature films "end." Typically. Sure, sometimes they tease a sequel or set up a franchise, but each entry tends to be a self-contained story brought to a satisfying climax, maybe with a denouement. Whereas episodic television is propelled, week after week — maybe even compelling binge-watching. This promise of the premise should be obvious from the logline. *What's the engine that drives your story?*

SITCOMS

Situation Comedies (sitcoms) rely on a setup requiring the consistent proximity of a regular cast of diametrically contrasted characters. A bit of a misnomer, they really ought to be called character comedies because all their stories are born out of the characters reacting to one another, triggered by the premise situation they are thrust into. Each episode scenario intentionally collides these divergent characters — socially, professionally but especially emotionally — in terms of worldviews and values to elicit the most conflict and thus, the greatest comedy.

PROCEDURALS

Procedural dramas have a built-in story engine. This could be a gurney barreling the story in through ER doors, delivering the case of the week or a dead body launching the crime story to be solved. The legal case that needs to be fought on behalf of a victim or a political scandal to unravel for some kind of client.

Similar to sitcoms, dramatic series are built upon strong main characters that live and work together within a specific milieu. Procedurals favor cops, lawyers and doctors because their lives have huge daily stakes. We're fascinated by the "process" that saves, protects or rebuilds lives.

Scripted Bible Guts

Series Overview

1 paragraph to 1 page.

Background on series concept.

Establish the franchise or setting.

Character Descriptions

1 page for all (or each) of the 3–5 main characters.

Include: backstory-defining moments, what brings them to the series'/season's/episode's plot, what inner conflicts do they struggle with, what makes them great? What flaws might be their downfall?

Weave the characters' interrelationships throughout your breakdowns. You could include images of a popular star whose personality (or that of the characters she's portrayed) reflects the character; or wardrobe reminiscent of the time period or world.

Pilot Treatment

4 –5 page synopsis.

Teaser/Cold Open

Intro the main character; tease the key conflict (e.g., if the teaser was a crime, then Act One might be the crime scene investigation), pose questions the episode will attempt to answer; end with a cliffhanger that will launch that episode and/or the whole series.

Act One

Flesh out the main episode characters, reveal the moral dilemma, ramp up the tension, deliver another cliffhanger.

Act Two	Similar to the second act in a movie, this is where the character will struggle with the conflict head on. This should feel like an uphill battle but with emerging hope. At the end of the act, flip expectations.
Act Three	Things derail, we're at a low point, our character is trapped or defeated. *What will happen? Is there any hope?*
Act Four	*Did she learn from mistakes made in the first two acts? Can she draw on her inner strength to resolve the conflict?*
Act Five	Often this is a wrap-up. Provide some additional closure, and perhaps tease out where the story will go next in future episodes. What future conflict is still to come? How was today's "win" just one battle in what looks more like it may be a war?
Future Episodes	2–3 sentence loglines (character, plot, subplot) for 4–12 of your best concepts. You could detail a few episodes of the first season, then just broad-stroke future plot milestones.
Future Seasons	Especially for serials, instead of detailing specific episodes, you could simply hit the major plot points in a paragraph or so about subsequent seasons, using mile markers

Mood Board

Contact Info

like "By mid-season. . ." and "Season One ends with. . ."

This could be a collage of style and tone images from your look book or you could pepper images throughout the entire bible (the world, key locations).

If you have the budget, hire an amazing graphic designer who's proficient with TV concepts. Or even a promising student. But if the art isn't great, don't use it — no matter what you paid for it or how close a family member the volunteer was.

TV Format Bibles

A TV format is the overall concept and branding of a TV franchise. Formats can be scripted[3] or unscripted ("reality"). Like a high-concept feature-film logline, if you can't get the essence across in a sentence to a very short paragraph, it's too complicated for a franchisable format.

Refine Your TV Format Genre Beyond Just "Reality"

Reality TV is one of the most competitive content categories in the global marketplace. But even within reality, there are game shows, competitions, factual, nonfiction, informative and documentary programming — the list goes on and on. And you have to know what it is you're pitching in order to find the right outlets and target audiences.

---

[3] Scripted pitch bibles are essentially the same regardless if targeted as franchisable formats.

Like scripted programming, reality television has definitive genre silos and narrative structures that are easily identified, described and reproduced. Distributors and viewers alike respond to repeatable formats. There's a simple beauty to producing and marketing them.

Formerly (and still often) referred to as "unscripted," this is a bit of a misnomer because so much of "reality" television is actually scripted. Not just the hosts' intros and outros or documentary voice-over narration, many of the shows' segments are artificially set up or re-enactments, if not outright staged.

Developing, producing and marketing truly original TV formats requires innovation. Whether you are pitching to attract development interest, a commissioning investment for your original concept or to license "in the can," market-ready content to territories around the world, you have to be able to pitch effectively — and that usually comes from putting in the work to develop the marketing materials that will help you get your project sold. But like features, you first need to define your genre — or TV format — so you're pitching the right content to the right outlets.

The Academy of Television Arts and Sciences (the entity that awards the Emmys) decided to break the Reality TV genre down into three loosely defined categories: Structured, Unstructured and Documentary. These definitions and which show falls into which category have evolved over time. . . and will continue to do so. Shows may shift from one category to another and new hybrids and categories will evolve. *Where does your project fit in?*

REALITY COMPETITION

The driving force of the reality boom, the four super formats all fall under reality competition. *Who Wants to Be a Millionaire?* is a game show. The *Idols* franchise falls squarely into the talent show (singing) category. *Survivor* is a structured reality competition show. *Big Brother* launched as a social experiment game show but evolved through negative publicity into the unstructured reality competition show it is today.

Reality competition has a competition element that awards a prize or title. Game shows are included in this category. From *Big Brother* or *Bachelor*-type homes, *Project Runway*, or *America's Next Top Model*–style dorms or *Temptation Island* tropical paradises, reality competition shows feature a camera-friendly cast with big personalities, in confined spaces, competing for substantial prizes. The pursuits range from extreme physical challenges such as obstacle courses or massive weight-loss to talent ranging from singing, dancing, cooking, fashion designing, cat walking and drag queening to simply dating or enduring roommates.

REALITY COMPETITION FORMAT EXAMPLES

- *Amazing Race* (CBS)
- *American Idol* (Fox)
- *American Ninja Warrior* (NBC)
- *The Apprentice* (NBC)
- *Dancing with the Stars* (ABC)
- *Last Comic Standing* (NBC)
- *Project Runway* (Lifetime)
- *RuPaul's Drag Race* (VH1)
- *Shark Tank* (ABC)
- *So You Think You Can Dance* (Fox)
- *Survivor* (CBS)
- *Top Chef* (Bravo)
- *The Voice* (NBC)

IN THE BEGINNING, TV CREATED THE GAME AND THE SHOW

Game shows were the first uniquely television-generated content. They led to amateur talent shows and are the antecedent of the whole reality competition genre.

> ## GAME SHOW FORMAT EXAMPLES
>
> - *Are You Smarter Than a Fifth Grader?*
> - *Deal or No Deal*
> - *Family Feud*
> - *The Hollywood Squares*
> - *Jeopardy!*
> - *Let's Make a Deal*
> - *Price Is Right*
> - *Weakest Link*
> - *Wheel of Fortune*
> - *Who Wants to Be a Millionaire?*

TALENT SHOWS

Talent competitions are reality TV's answer to features and scripted Heroes' Journeys. These shows pluck average "Janes" out of their everyday lives and thrust them onto a national stage for us to watch with fascination, not unlike the gladiators of yore, as they accept challenges, overcome obstacles and contend with failure.

Audience identification works much the same way as it does in scripted. To create empathy and rooting interest, the contestants' backstories are doled out to us in increasingly involved snippets the further up the rankings they make it.

Contestants elevate themselves based on their own merits, in front of a panel of judges or up for public vote, for rewards they alone will reap. The weekly elimination process adds suspense and unpredictability to keep viewers glued to the screen, tweeting, posting and voting — but most of all: tuning back in.

"And . . . ACTION!"
Creative Reality Competition
Format Challenge

Come up with a TV format that, instead of changing the life of just one winner, makes the world a better place. Develop a game that is entertaining while it rewards collaboration over competition, brains over brawn and engages similar elevated participation from the audience at home.

STRUCTURED REALITY

Structured reality programs typically put characters into pre-arranged scenarios — without scripting their dialogue — but with consistent story elements that adhere to a recurring template. There is usually some sort of a routine. The format is front and center, very straightforward.

STRUCTURED REALITY TV DOMAINS

Court Cases	Outdoor Survival
Crafts	Paranormal
Event Planning (wedding, etc.)	Renovation
Hidden Camera	Self-Improvement
Home Search	Social Experiment
Makeover	Supernatural

STRUCTURED REALITY TV SHOW EXAMPLES

Antiques Roadshow (PBS)	*MythBusters* (Discovery)
Catfish (MTV)	*Pawn Stars* (History)
Deadliest Catch (Discovery Channel)	*Queer Eye* (Netflix)
Dog Whisperer with Cesar Milan (National Geographic)	*Queer Eye for the Straight Guy* (Bravo)
Extreme Makeover: Home Edition (ABC)	*Shark Tank* (ABC)
Fixer Upper (HGTV)	*Undercover Boss* (CBS)
Lip Sync Battle (Paramount)	*Who Do You Think You Are?* (TLC)

PROCESS/BUILD SHOWS

Process or build shows have a game plan: You lay out the parameters and we see what happens. As an example, *in Ace of Cakes*, every week we follow three cakes — whatever happens, happens. It feels as real as possible. Each setup is deliberate but their outcomes are not controlled.

▶ *Legal/Crime*

Legal or crime-related shows follow a process: a court case, bounty hunters' pursuits, repossession adventures, cold-case crime investigations, reenactments, prison journeys, etc.

Hot Tip! Keep your premise concise. Build the series in a way that tells the story in an efficient but satisfying manner. Distinguish and mold substantial steps. Ensure each episode pays off with some sort of victory or new discovery — then break each episode down into chunks.

▶ *Cooking*

Cooking shows are very talent-based. It's rare to get one off the ground without either a celebrity chef or an exciting new one. Notable format twists include shows like *Ready Steady Cook* (BBC) that pair celebrity chefs with everyday audience members in fun cooking competitions.

▶ *Prank*

Prank shows are all about the twist. There have been so many different variations of *Candid Camera* over the years, if you're going to build a hidden camera show, you have to explore new subjects or territory that hasn't already been tackled in the past. There have been versions for those with disabilities, seniors, parents pranking their kids, magicians pranking the public — you have to come up with something new.

Hot Tip! Prank shows are incredibly specialist. There's a very specific approach to doing prank shows and once you've pitched one — and made one — it's much easier to get others set up. Thus, aligning with a proven production company in this realm is likely critical (unless you have those kinds of credits under your belt).

▶ *Transformation/Self-Improvement*
Self-awareness shows involve a major lifestyle change such as eliminating a self-destructive habit, attitude or addiction and are often accompanied by professional support such as psychiatrists, psychologists, private trainers, nutritionists, home health chefs, professional organizers, image consultants, plastic surgeons — or teams of experts.

▶ *Social Experiment*
Social experiment shows challenge traditional social structures and put everyday people into extreme situations so the audience can watch how the drama unfolds. *Wife Swap, Married at First Sight, Naked and Afraid* are a few good examples.

▶ *Travel*
Travel shows often include discovering little-seen places, often with an element of danger and adventure, like *Anthony Bourdain: Parts Unknown* (CNN). Destination or resort shows are often sponsored by a hotel chain or travel company.

UNSTRUCTURED REALITY

Unstructured reality programs don't have a consistent template. They typically follow a continuing cast of real-life characters who drive the action, with the focus being on their reactions and interactions rather than a set story line.

UNSTRUCTURED REALITY TV SHOW EXAMPLES

- *Antiques Roadshow* (PBS)
- *Born This Way* (A&E)
- *Deadliest Catch* (Discovery Channel)
- *Dirty Jobs* (Discovery Channel)
- *Flipping Out* (Bravo)
- *Gaycation with Ellen Page* (Viceland)
- *Hoarders* (A&E)
- *Intervention* (A&E)
- *Kathy Griffin: My Life on the D-List* (Bravo)
- *Million Dollar Listing* (Bravo)
- *Naked and Afraid* (Discovery Channel)
- *Penn & Teller: Bullshit!* (Showtime)
- *Project Greenlight* (HBO)
- *RuPaul's Drag Race: Untucked* (VH1)
- *Taxicab Confessions* (HBO)
- *The Osbournes* (MTV)
- *United Shades of America With W. Kamau Bell* (CNN)
- *Wahlburgers* (A&E)

LIFESTYLE/DOCUSOAP

Unstructured lifestyle/docusoap reality shows follow large personalities around their daily lives and track what unfolds. There has been criticism that many of the situations, relationships and scenarios are trumped up to jack up the drama.

LIFESTYLE/DOCUSOAP EXAMPLES

- *Duck Dynasty* (A&E)
- *Keeping Up with the Kardashians* (E!)
- *Little Women* franchise (Lifetime)
- *The Real Housewives* franchise (Bravo)

▶*A Day in the Life of . . .*

An "up close and personal," almost voyeuristic glimpse into how fascinating characters live their lives. Or at least how people navigate rarified vocations or avocations such as border security agents, tattoo artists, assorted specialists, training for competitive events, etc.

The distinction between "A Day in the Life of. . ." unstructured reality elements versus "Men at Work" "produced nonfiction content" isn't clear. Perhaps the difference is the former could be self-contained episodes, each on different characters or worlds versus "an ongoing documentary process" on one or a cast of characters or a specific milieu — but it's hazy.

DOCUMENTARY/NONFICTION SPECIALS AND SERIES

Documentary or nonfiction specials and series are in-depth, investigational programs with a unified story and overall show arc, substantively comprised of documentary elements or produced nonfiction content.

Our voracious appetite for meaningful human connection through factual edutainment has driven a dynamic renaissance in documentary programming. Documentarians have to be great storytellers: part journalist, part filmmaker.

Docs are all about access: following interesting people around with cameras rolling, chronicling their daily events, interviewing subjects, victims, perpetrators, politicians, eye witnesses, subject-matter experts, local-color characters. Like modern media archaeologists, producers must unearth the story. They have to dig through bins of shot footage, mountains of research materials, archived photos, journals and letters to discover their story spine and refine their unifying theme. The story often emerges or evolves, sometimes totally morphing from the original battle plan.

Docs require time to simmer creatively. Producers have to have the financial wherewithal to follow some stories for years.

They are ultimately all about pacing but they don't conform to TV schedules or budgets, which are always so tight. This can be particularly dangerous territory because you're often following a story that unfolds slowly, often erratically — and you have no idea how it'll play out.

With salvage shows, it could take a crew two to three years to raise a shipwreck — and they might not find any treasure. With process shows, you might have to wait and follow a trial as it plays out in the criminal justice system.

 TIP: Let's say you're tracking police detectives over three years and the case takes them to twenty-seven different places. Boil all their footage down to the five or six most important or interesting leads. Simplify. Just like in features: compress time, condense cast.

MEN-AT-WORK DOCUMENTARIES

Men-at-work docs, like *Ice Road Truckers* (History), launched the beginning of the reality craze. This genre is particularly trend-driven.

Some of the distinctions between documentary/nonfiction and reality TV are that to qualify for the former, any re-creations, including the use of performers or animation, must be fact-based and used for illustration purposes only. Any set-up environments or events must be used exclusively to disseminate factual information without reality elements.

 ### "And . . . ACTION!"
Google Reality Comps Winners & Nods

Google for the past Emmy and NATPE Reality Breakthrough Awards nominees and winners in unstructured reality, structured reality and reality competition. Study the best in your class. Reverse engineer why and how they connected with audiences and the industry. Parlay that knowledge to help your creation compete with the cream of the crop.

Children's Programming

Every demographic has its stratum but few are as dramatically delineated as kids' television programming because the distinctions between age groups are so profound. The difference in comprehension levels between a twenty-three-year-old and a twenty-six-year-old is minor. The difference between three- and six-year-olds is major.

Preschool and the six-to-twelve age categories are the target demographics for most children's channels but many broadcasters are returning to the challenges of creating age-appropriate drama for eleven- to sixteen-year-olds.

Preschool audiences favor strong, relatable, believable characters. They become the child's friend. For older kids, friendship is still fundamental but action and humor become major factors in capturing children's imaginations. For boys aged six to nine, there has been a shift away from action adventure to engaging with comedy.

Some of the cornerstones of children's programming are friendship, fantastical adventures, humor, stimulating the imagination and exploring the broad principles of science and nature through creative play, crafting and invention. Event-led and holiday themes tend to work well for home entertainment. Interstitials or short "in between" complementary companion content that demonstrate how to create things children have seen on the show can augment series concepts.

"And . . . ACTION!"
Creative Kids' Programming Challenge

There is a global effort to attract girls to STEAM (Science, Technology, Engineering, the Arts and Math) industries. Come up with a concept to inspire children to start exploring how things are made, how things work and the world around them.

But . . . Will it Travel?

A key first step to selling a format is to ensure your idea is international enough to appeal to global markets.

Marriage and family issues are fairly universal and evergreen. While history can be a safe perennial topic, it can be a tough sell because history is so geographically and culturally rooted. Science tends to be borderless. And every country loves music.

The reality competition amateur talent show *The Voice*, originally a Dutch format, has been adapted in 145 territories. A really easy-to-understand concept: blind auditions, contingent on singing quality alone. Top artists in the music industry hit a buzzer and spin around in rotating chairs to see what kind of a character had such a terrific voice that they have sight-unseen committed to mentor. Originally designed to compete with *The X Factor*, the show's protectable format features five competition phases: producers' auditions, blind auditions, battle rounds, knockouts (since 2012) and live performance competitions as well as a great deal of social media interactivity.

Local Success First

One of the best ways to get a format to travel is to create a local success first — ideally one that gets picked up as an international story and has an easy-to-adapt production setup.

The world has flattened. Strive for formats that can be reproduced with local talent in local languages according to their local cultures.

Proposals & Business Plans

Proposals present a unique value proposition, customized to a specific prospect, with a unique call to action. Whereas pitch packages are specific to the project, proposals are the step between pitch packages and business plans. Containing largely the same content as the former, proposals don't disclose all the numbers as a presentation to an equity investor would. Often used for advertising, product placement, vendor joint ventures, like business plans, proposals preemptively answer anticipated questions to convince the target audience to engage in the opportunity.

Once you move beyond proposing content for others to make to soliciting investment to facilitate your producing the work, then you move past pitching a product into pitching a business venture. That's when you need a business plan. And just as a script is the blueprint for the cinematic story, your business *plan* is the blueprint for its manufacture and dissemination. They can be as creative as scripts, tweaked as many times and should be customized to your target audience.

The Ask

Your prospect doesn't have ESP. Don't make them do the heavy lifting, guessing what it is you want from them. Be clear about your expectations and what your end goal is. What — exactly — are you "proposing"? Stay focused on who it's going to and what you want them to do as a result of reviewing your materials.

What Do You Want?

Proposals
- ❑ A Co-Production Partner?
- ❑ Product Placement? Cash?
- ❑ Affinity Marketing Support?
- ❑ Soundtrack/Score/Music Licensing?

Business Plans
- ❑ Equity Investment?

Proposal Elements

IDENTIFY YOUR TARGET AUDIENCE

Assure your prospect that your *accessible* target audience over-laps with their demographics. Develop profiles — or avatars, if you will — that might be representative of the different market segments and affinity groups your project should appeal to. Strategize how you might position marketing to them. *What channels do they watch? What festivals or events do they attend? Who might you be able to partner with to cross-promote? Who might be your social media ambassadors? How well do you know the fans of your genre?*

"And . . . ACTION!"
Reverse Engineer Your Target
Demographics to Seed Your Prospect Hit List

Who has the same target audience as you? What channels, shows, brands or periodicals target the same demographics? Look at their ads. What watches, shoes or glasses does your target audience wear? What food or beverage brands would your characters binge? What kind of car would your characters — or audience members — drive? Make a list. Check it thrice.

The Schedule

It's prudent to have a production schedule on a list of documents available upon request but you don't have to include that in your business plan, certainly not in a proposal.

While the schedule can dictate every moment of principal photography, it's usually more minutia than most equity investors might be interested in. Just as confusion can jar your script readers from being engaged with your characters, so too can your investors' interest be dislodged by unnecessary or unfamiliar detail.

	Scenes: 9	EXT	MOUNTAIN RANGE	2/8 pgs.	CAST IDs: VEHICLE IDs:
	Scenes: 10	EXT	MOUNTAIN	2/8 pgs.	CAST IDs: VEHICLE IDs:
	Scenes: 1	EXT	COUNTRY ROAD	1/8 pgs.	CAST IDs: VEHICLE IDs:
	Scenes: 6	EXT	COUNTRY ROAD	1/8 pgs.	CAST IDs: VEHICLE IDs:
	Scenes: 3	EXT	BRIDGE	3/8 pgs.	CAST IDs: 4, 6, 7 VEHICLE IDs:
	Scenes: 7	EXT	BRIDGE	2/8 pgs.	CAST IDs: 4 VEHICLE IDs:
MEAL BREAK					
	Scenes: 5	EXT	GRAY SEDAN	2/8 pgs.	CAST IDs: VEHICLE IDs:
	Scenes: 2	INT	GRAY SEDAN	1/8 pgs.	CAST IDs: 6, 7 VEHICLE IDs:
	Scenes: 4	INT	GRAY SEDAN	3/8 pgs.	CAST IDs: 6 VEHICLE IDs:
	Scenes: 8	INT	BLACK ELECTRIC VAN	5/8 pgs.	CAST IDs: 4, 6 VEHICLE IDs:
End of Shooting Day 5 -- Friday, June 7, 2019 -- 2 6/8 Pages					
	Scenes: 11	INT	BLACK SITE PRISON - TORTURE ROOM	2 4/8 pgs.	CAST IDs: 1, 5 VEHICLE IDs:
	Scenes: 13	INT	BLACK SITE PRISON - TORTURE ROOM	1/8 pgs.	CAST IDs: 1 VEHICLE IDs:
	Scenes: 15	INT	BLACK SITE PRISON - TORTURE ROOM	3/8 pgs.	CAST IDs: 1, 5 VEHICLE IDs:
	Scenes: 19	INT	BLACK SITE PRISON	4/8 pgs.	CAST IDs: 1, 3 VEHICLE IDs:
MEAL BREAK					
	Scenes: 16	INT	BLACK SITE PRISON - CELL	3/8 pgs.	CAST IDs: 1 VEHICLE IDs:
	Scenes: 18	INT	BLACK SITE PRISON - CELL	2 2/8 pgs.	CAST IDs: 1, 3, 5 VEHICLE IDs:
End of Shooting Day 6 -- Monday, June 10, 2019 -- 6 1/8 Pages					

To the uninitiated, traditional production strip boards can be initially intimidating and difficult to comprehend. Just give them the big picture. They want to be able to wrap their minds around what's anticipated to be going on when, where — and maybe why. A table with a simple summary of tasks (beyond

Breaking News Proposed Procuction Schedule	
ASAP	Secure Financing
Week 1	SET-UP: Open 2-signature bank account (Private Equity Investor + one other team member), retain entertainment attorney, prepare all legal docs, form LLC, negotiate with Casting Director, submit for tax incentives.
Week 2	SOFT PREP: 1st Draft of the Screenplay delivered to PEI & CD, vet prioritized cast wish list with core territory ISAs, polish first pass schedule and production budget, share cast breakdowns with talent agents.
Weeks 3 & 4	PRE-PRODUCTION: Audtion / attach key cast, talent polishes to script, interview Department Heads and hire Keys, produce preliminary key art, design social media campaign, polish 2nd draft of the screenplay, set up production offices.
Week 5	PRE-PRODUCTION:Location scout w/DP and Production Designer, storyboard complicated sequences, polish and lock shooting script.
Week 6 - 7	PRODUCTION: Hire balance of crew, secure equipment, location/logistics polish to script, build website, launch social media campaign w/Director's Diary and Dept. Head vlogs.
Weeks 8 - 12	PRINCIPAL PHOTOGRAPHY Estimated to be 25-day shoot of five 5-day work weeks
W8	INT. STUDIO - NEWS DESK SET: Anchor desk, BTS studio floor [set-up to hold-up]
W9-10	INT. STUDIO: Follow each ensemble characters' POV (one day per storyline experience) through make-up, green room, edit bays, crawl spaces, hostage holding rooms, etc.
W11	EXT. STUDIO COMPLEX: Main love story scenes, thriller transitional interaction elements, storage rooms, warehouse, etc.
W12	EXT.: house and park scenes, B-Roll, pick-ups
Months 4 - 8	POST-PRODUCTION; Edit, finalize key art, prepare festival campaign strategy (Midnight Madness premiere at the Toronto Int'l Film Fest or band party premiere with booze sponsor at SXSW (sell schwag and soundtrack)
Month 10	RELEASE: Streaming Launch, cascading event marketing affinity distribution, mainstream ad campaign

just the principal photography shoot), might give a more meaningful overview of the entire production. Keep it easy on the eyes and quickly comprehensible.

Logistics change. And while a projected start date can prove to be a rallying elixir, to avoid having to constantly update these documents, consider ballparking weeks. If an investor wants you to commit to actual calendar dates. . . *can you imagine an edit you'd rather make?*

Budget

If you're pitching to a production company, you won't likely include a budget (or even a budget figure). More likely — if they're interested — they will break your script or concept down into a proposed schedule and tell *you* what the budget should be.

If your proposal is to coproduce the project, that is a number you should agree on together.

If you're pitching to a joint venture partner, only that department's budget should be relevant to them. But if they ask to see the whole thing, it will depend on how transparent you want to be with them, and what the risks — or upsides — are in revealing it to them.

If you're pitching to a distributor or a brand, it's actually none of their business what your movie or television content cost — just what it's worth to them.

If you don't have a budget — or know how to create one or have the budget to hire someone to do break it down for you — but are pressed to pull a number out of the air, reverse engineer your financial comps to determine the sweet spot of where your budget *should be*.

An equity investor, of course, has a right to know how, when and where her money's going to be spent — and how much more she'll get back (and when). Just as your logline heads off your one sheet, the top sheet of your budget should be sufficient for your business plan. But it should be fully backed by a full-blown, line-itemed budget — which can often exceed fifty pages. And if you're pitching, you should understand every line item.

Cast Wish Lists and Talent Attachments

Castability runs neck and neck with high concept. Fantastic characters that attract terrific actors is a coveted quality, one that creates an exponential magnetizing effect. Even though there isn't a strong correlation between star power and box office performance, recognizable faces give private equity investors, distributors, international sales agents and television outlets marketing comfort. It eases their concerns that respected professionals have already vetted and endorsed your project by committing to star in it.

Name talent typically attracts talented peers, thus raising the quality of the performances of the entire cast. Thus, the marketplace success is more likely due to high-quality acting heightening production value than marquee value (but try telling anyone in financing or distribution that).

Whereas in a pitch package, you reveal the essence of the main *characters* as written, in a proposal, you might suggest *casting* strategies. Casting really well-known talent has the most significant statistical impact on independent dramas budgeted between $1 million and $10 million.

Every project benefits from the right cast, but if your project is cast-contingent — if you need stars to make your project work — the Powers That Be are certain to question the merits of your concept or story.

Attachments may make key players more receptive to your pitch, but if the names aren't meaningful they become an obstacle. Actually, studios and triple-letter agencies often prefer high-concept projects with zero attachments so they have the freedom to package. A prudent targeted proposal might customize suggestions exclusively within a prospective agent's or manager's stable, allowing reps and their companies to not only envision the constellations of internally contracted possibilities but incentivize them by multiple layers of potential commissions.

If you already have actors attached, use either their most flattering, current headshot or a recent production still of a character reminiscent of their intended role. Highlight their IMDbPro STARmeter ranking, Vscore or their Numbers Bankability Index. Detail their social media footprint: how many fans and followers they have on key platforms — and how active they are (or their team is).

And certainly, *don't* detail who *was* attached in the past or who's considering attaching. Either they're attached or they're not. The list of those who've moved on or passed just diminishes your project's value if it's been dog-eared all over town and still no one's made it. Yes, of course: many legendary blockbuster successes fall into this category. We're not talking about fairness here. We're talking perception. Marketplace reality.

MATERIAL		MARKETS
Treatment	←∞→	Script (Feature or TV)
Bible	←∞→	TV Series
Format Bible	←∞→	TV Franchise
Proposal	←∞→	Joint Venture Opportunity
Business Plan	←∞→	Equity Investment Opportunity

Video Marketing Assets

In an industry of multimedia pros with compressed attention spans, accustomed to big budget moving images, if a picture is worth a thousand words, then video is worth a million. Video presentations are used at each stage of the development and marketing process, from business-to-business pitching to direct-to-consumer advertising. Where you're at in the development process will dictate what raw assets you have at your disposal. Your technical expertise as well as your financial, equipment and logistical resources will determine what you can do with them.

But if video production isn't your realm of expertise, it's often better to stick to words on the page because the bar is raised so high for the professionalism, quality and production value. If your core skill-set lies in literary mastery, rely on that to conjure their bigger-budgeted imaginations. Don't diminish your credibility by showing cheesy, low-quality footage with unknowns that will certainly destroy any hopeful expectations.

Independent production companies can spend a couple hundred thousand dollars on sizzle reels — and a tenth of that on advertising agencies' slick graphical leave-behinds — never to recoup a penny. Individual content creators rarely have such deep pockets, crew or post-production resources at the ready. And some that do rely on pretty pictures and empty promises to spackle weaknesses blatantly obvious to professionals in the biz.

But executives love visuals. Footage can be invaluable. And anything that speeds up the process is welcome. *Do you have the technical skills, equipment, contacts or financial resources to pull together a video presentation?* If that effort is economically feasible and commensurate with the odds of the opportunity, tape *might* be the difference that gets you and your project noticed. Visually conveying the cinematics might be the tipping point that gets your calls and emails returned, gets you into the right rooms — and maybe even gets you a deal inked.

A sizzle reel that is :30 – 2:30 in length, a 3:00–5:00 talent reel, or even a 7:00 polished segment can make or break a pitch — or get you one. Whatever video elements you use, make sure you only select the highest production-value clips you have to offer. When in doubt, throw it out. Less is more. Far better to have thirty amazing seconds that compel commitment versus forty-five that include one weak clip that inspires second thoughts or squelches the impulse of interest.

Teaser

Teasers are the first sneak peek of a film, used to create audience anticipation. Typically :20–1:30, these initial glimpses may be the first footage available, exploiting the star power of famous actors or the credibility of established filmmakers while the film is still in production.

Teasers may not actually reveal any footage from the film at all. They could just be silhouettes, special effects or a costume establishing the mood or tone. Think *Batman*: the iconic bat-signal over a Gotham skyline, the cool new Batmobile or the new superhero cast in the mask and cape.

Rarely chronological and often without giving away any plot details, teasers highlight the main idea. All about the mystery, their goal is to pique curiosity, whet the audience's appetite and leave them wanting more. Starting months before the release date, teasers often project the season ("next Christmas" or "Halloween 2022") or month the film will be released.

Theatrical Trailer

Closer to the actual premiere, trailers are commercials for a completed film made up exclusively of the funniest and most exciting film clips edited together, usually in story order, that introduce the main character and reveal a lot of the plot (some would argue, spoiling any surprise).

The name comes from when these commercials trailed after the main feature to entice audiences to come back to the cinema in the future to see what was "Coming Soon." Now they are shown before the movie and usually give the exact release date.

Trailers can also be as short as :30. The maximum length is 2:30, as established by the Motion Picture Association of America. But each studio or distributor may exceed this limitation for one film per year, usually their tentpole entry.

"And . . . ACTION!"
Script Your Trailer

Try writing a two-column script with visuals on the left and audio (dialogue, music, sound effects) on the right. Keep each "beat" aligned by row. *Can you get all the key turning points of your story concept in thirty seconds? Or two-and-a-half minutes? Without giving the ending away? Does imagining your potential trailer reveal any plot holes or missed opportunities in your script?*

"And . . . ACTION!"
Study Your Comps' Trailers

Watch your comps' trailers. *Do you recognize any consistent elements or patterns? How does yours diverge? Can you make it even more unique?*

"And . . . ACTION!"
Study Award-Winning Trailers
in Your Genre

Check out *HeatherHale.com/StorySelling* for the latest trailer award-winners from:

- Golden Trailer
- Trailer Addict
- CableFax.com

Does studying some of the current greats give you any brainstorm breakthroughs? Do they give you any ideas of how you might be able to make your script more cinematic? Or exciting? Or emotional?

Re-Cut Trailers Inspire Genre Insight

Art begets art. Along the lines of the cliché "imitation is the sincerest form of flattery," re-cut trailers edit original trailers into entirely different genres, usually for comedic effect, sometimes for pure creep factor. Reimagine *The Shining* as a romantic comedy, *Jaws* as a Disney musical, *Mrs. Doubtfire* as a psychological thriller, *Mary Poppins* and *Willie Wonka* as horror movies and *The Ten Commandments* as a teen comedy. These parody mash-ups lift footage from the source trailer (or other moments in the film), separate the audio and video tracks, strip the clips of the mood-defining score or soundtrack and replace it with completely different music to change the feeling and context to a rewritten and freshly recorded voice-over narration.

As the barriers to entry in the film and television industry continue to plunge, virtually everyone has an editing suite at home — and can learn to use it. But they also offer an interesting way to study how putting the pieces together in a different way could lead to marketing an entirely different work of art.

"And . . . ACTION!"
Compare Re-Cut Trailers to
Their Originals

HeatherHale.com/StorySelling has links to many, or just Google for plenty.

"And . . . ACTION!"
Re-Trailer of One of Your Comps

This is purely for fun. And genre exploration. Stretching your creative muscles. Looking at your work inside out and upside down. This could be simply a paper edit: Re-order the clips they used and script a different narration in an A/V script. Or try your hand at actually editing a trailer for one of your favorite films or TV shows into a different genre. *Does even just paying*

more attention to "trailer moments" and obligatory scenes
give you a fresh new perspective for your project?

Sizzle Reel

Sizzle reels are usually trailers for projects that don't exist yet, to help your prospect visualize how your project might be marketed if it were already in the can, "as if" they were watching a trailer for a series that already exists. It helps them visualize not only the look and feel of the premise as it unfolds in action but it also sets the bar for your professionalism.

For a feature film or television show, this could actually be a few trailer moments actually staged and shot. (Some samples are on this book's companion website, *HeatherHale.com/Story-Selling*). Some filmmakers shoot short films with the intention of editing them into a sizzle reel to pitch the longer work. It might include stock footage mixed with rip-o-matic scenes.

For speculative reality TV projects or documentaries, where you're not building sets or casting actors but are rather capturing real people in real locations, it can be a little easier to get some on-location tease footage, maybe even some preemptive interviews to convey the personalities and world.

Sell the Sizzle, Not the Steak

You write the words but you pitch the feelings. Sizzles can help you sell that emotion in a crisp, visually appealing way. Keep these videos around :30–2:30.

Sizzle reels often accompany unscripted series pitch packages or format bibles. They are all about the tease, conjuring the potential in your prospect's mind's eye. TV is intimate.

Animated Sizzle Reel

Animated sizzle reels can be a terrific solution for a lot of reality programming. Cleverly written, they can be especially effective to lay out the mechanics of a game show format, animating words for quiz shows. Big physical challenges can be especially cost-prohibitive to shoot but animated schematics intermixed with internet footage and stills can cost-effectively offer a sense of these bigger shows within reasonable stakes for all parties.

Rip-O-Matic

A "rip-o-matic" is a short business-to-business pitching video, edited together from footage literally "ripped off" from comparable or relevant movies, television and other video sources.

Usually unified by music, sometimes by voice-over narration, often interspersed with some of the original dialogue and sound effects, this mock-up borrows the production value and star quality of preexisting genre clips to portray an emotionally engaging glimpse of the intended look and feel of the proposed project. Rarely shared publicly (to avoid any potential copyright infringement issues), these are behind-closed-sales-doors (or at industry events) business-to-business pitching tools.

Rip-o-matics are terrific tools to pitch your independent film to prospective equity investors or your TV series concept to brands and their agencies. Visit: *HeatherHale.com/Story-Selling* for samples.

"And . . . ACTION!"
Edit Your Comps into a Rip-O-Matic
for Your Project

What are the moments from among your comps that jumped out at you as relevant to the current project you're pitching? Make a list of those moments and align them with the A/V trailer script you wrote earlier. *Are you missing pieces? Too many holes?*

Another approach is to take the two or three best comps that your project is a cross of and edit together the pieces into your own Frankenstein-like rip-o-matic — on the page or in an editing program. Or get an editing buddy to help you. *What're the beats you're missing? What would the voice-over narration be? If any? Could on-screen graphics or titles cover missing pieces? Do any of these marketing efforts drive you back to rewrite your script? Or come up with new, more marketable ideas?*

Talent Reels

With unscripted content, getting tape on reality talent can be priceless. Tape takes the idea off the page to the next level. On-location footage of your characters in their most visually interesting milieus, applying their skills and expertise in an emotionally engaging way, can reveal the personalities, compelling activities, intimate moments and potential conflicts the show promises while the format of the sizzle or talent reel can suggest the proposed structure of the show.

Sometimes potential talent is so uniquely intriguing that two different versions of a talent reel might be developed: one a character-based iteration that plays up the docu-elements while an alternate, super-formatted expression will be re-sequenced with different cards to highlight the format points.

If you're a subject-matter expert, footage can help production companies wrap their minds around what a potential reality TV show starring or hosted by you might look and feel like.

Completed Scenes

At film markets (not festivals), if you have a completed movie, a consumer-type trailer is great. But if your project is still in production or post, five minutes of selected completed scenes can do wonders to get professionals to start tracking your project and be receptive to status updates.

Acquisition executives like to see completed scenes to get a feel for the pace and tone of the film. Select a few key scenes and post them on a website so your distributors and sales companies can view them before committing to a meeting. Links can go in your emails without the worry of attachments being too large or rejected. Burn a few DVDs with your trailer and completed scenes to facilitate clicking on the precise moment you want to share for in-person meetings.

Frankenbiting

Reality TV often edits together clips of different moments and especially reactions to make one conversation, often drastically changing the context or rhythm. Sometimes this even involves reshoots of coached delivery in staged scenarios. While engaging spotting practice for continuity mistake junkies, "Frankenbiting" leaves many unscripted viewers unsatiated, seeking genuine moments of humanity that haven't been constructed or manipulated offscreen.

Still, for the purposes of getting across the most amount of emotion and conflict in the shortest amount of time, this might serve to amp up the tension and excitement of your pitching materials.

Proof of Concept

Some aspirants shoot short films or web series to demonstrate they can professionally execute their feature film or TV series idea. This can be an efficient and effective way to illustrate not only the concept, vision, character and worlds — but any unique storytelling techniques. This can be a terrific calling-card strategy, especially for writer/directors.

For reality, confessionals can be utilized as a narrative device to clearly depict characters and explore their proposed inter-relationships and the stakes involved but also to weave the stories together. In three to five minutes, you can show what the locations look like, how each episode will be formatted, any consistent episode elements you intend to employ as well as show off your ability to deliver on the promise of your pitch.

Dirty Pilot

A "dirty pilot" is a halfway step between a trailer, teaser or talent reel and an actual full-blown pilot. Further proof of concept, this could perhaps be an open and two acts of a show, with all the elements of that segment, including: intros, outros, theme music, graphics, etc. A successful pitch can sometimes result in an outlet commissioning a "dirty pilot," essentially ordering a partial trial run to see how good it turns out.

"And . . . ACTION!"
Script a Hypothetical Pilot of the First Two Acts of Your Reality Show

Game Show Proof-of-Concept Pilot

Game show proof-of-concept pilots used to be more common. Producers would speculatively spend their own money to hire actors to demonstrate their game play. But shooting a pilot before the broadcaster is engaged and has had an opportunity to share any input can prove to be a false economy. It's less financially onerous to limit development expense — not to mention the pressure on the commissioner.

Screener

Screeners are the actual, completed film or television program on a CD, DVD or online digital format. Password-protected websites such as Cinando allow independent filmmakers to pitch to distribution companies and international sales agents prior to or at markets. Festival platforms such as *FilmFreeway. com* allow for submissions to contests.

PITCHING

Pitching is actually quite simple. It's achieving mastery at it that's a challenge.

Like sports, music, art, languages or any other skill worth acquiring, practice leads to proficiency. This often leads to enjoyment, sometimes even enhanced professional and financial success — reminiscent of Picasso's napkin. If you're not familiar with the legend: The eminent artist was purportedly sitting at a bar when a woman offered to pay him to draw something. After casually dashing off a sketch, Picasso demanded a prodigious price. Balking, she protested it only took him a few seconds. Crumpling up the napkin and putting it in his shirt pocket, Picasso corrected her: *No, it took me forty years.*

Similarly, pitches belie the inordinate amount of disciplined development and preparation it takes to come across as relaxed and improvisational. Like great jazz, a good pitch should radiate spontaneity, creative freedom and love for the content and its expression.

But that expertise is earned. Through practice. Just as Olympians' and professional athletes' arduous journeys of hard work and sacrifice just to *get* to the starting block are judged in seconds to minutes, there is so much focus on the pitch itself when in reality, 95% of the real work is done before the pitch even starts. Ideally, as invisible and enjoyable in its execution as a magic trick.

There Are No Rules
(*and They Are Strictly Enforced*)

One of the things that makes the pitching process cumbersome for the uninitiated is that there is no "proper protocol" — but everyone knows when it's "wrong." Ever been to a conference with a live pitch event? Eight hundred audience members know instantly — painful minutes before the pitcher usually clues in — that the pitch has lost its way. It can be uncomfortable for all when laughter doesn't come when expected. Or worse: when it comes when not intended.

So much of the development and marketing work done is actually pitch preparation as well. But figuring out who to pitch to — and how — is another huge part of the preparatory battle.

Prospecting

Prospecting is a fine art. Those 5 W questions —*Who? What? Why? Where? When?* — aren't only the building blocks of your actual pitch; they are the milestones of the entire pitching process as well. Not just the five questions of the intellectual property you're offering up — but of each pitch prospect and new opportunity, too. *Who are you pitching to? What are you pitching? Where, when, why and how? What are they looking for?* (Research and development.) *How might you deliver exactly that to secure — and close — a deal with them?* (Marketing and sales.)

Marketing comps are one of the best ways to reverse engineer the beginnings of a prospecting list. These are the footprints left behind by your most obvious leads. You already know that whoever produced, distributed or financed your comps shares at least some creative sensibilities with you and this project. It doesn't necessarily mean they're interested in doing another similar project but. . . they've at least been involved in something similar before — and they might share your tastes or interests enough to do another. Comps help you zero in on the successful players in a given genre or format and help you identify priority candidates.

"And . . . ACTION!"
Reverse Engineer Your Comps Lists to Seed Your Prospect Hit List(s)

Study who produced, financed, distributed — even starred in or directed — your creative and marketing comps. *Do any names dominate the list? Any intriguing candidates emerge?*

Speed Tour of the "Buyer" Landscape

It can be tough to have the bandwidth for all of this but if you don't have an agent, manager or an experienced producer or team helming your project, you are your own development department.

If the Pareto Principle is accurate, and 20% of the industry is responsible for 80% of its production, the more you can home in on who your most viable prospects might be, the less you'll spin your wheels pitching to entities who couldn't help you even if they said "Yes!" The happy dance after a successful pitch, celebrating signing with a rep or optioning your work is short-lived if they do nothing to move you or your work forward.

Below is a simplified snapshot of the ever-changing landscape and best points of entry.

The "Big Five" Studios

Eighty-five percent of the United States media market is controlled by five major diversified media conglomerates that are all within 15 miles of one another in the Los Angeles area:

1. Walt Disney Pictures (Walt Disney Studios acquired 20th Century Fox in 2019)
2. Warner Bros. Pictures (WarnerMedia/AT&T)
3. Universal Pictures (NBCUniversal/Comcast)
4. Columbia Pictures (Sony Pictures)
5. Paramount Pictures (Viacom)

Most media is funded, distributed or marketed through one of their tentacles. But you probably wouldn't want to pitch directly to them for a myriad of reasons. Aside from their being nearly impenetrable, even if you could get in to pitch to them and didn't get lost in the shuffle, you'd be limited to six all-or-nothing, high-pressure, hole-in-one swings versus 1,000+ tee shots. Far better to approach a far more accessible point of entry that has a preexisting professional working relationship with them to get in play.

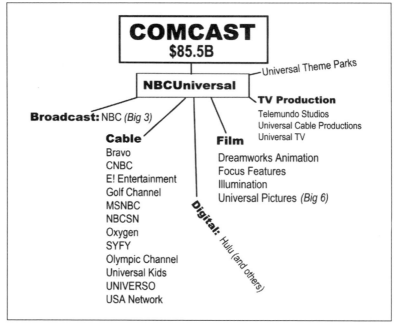

Simplified illustration of one of the Big Six vertically-integrated media conglomerates.

NBCUniversal, a subsidiary of Comcast, has one broadcast, twelve cable and several digital networks, four film and three TV production companies, multiple theme parks, among many other holdings.

Mini Majors

The next powerhouse tier is the "Mini Majors," including (among others):

- Lionsgate
- Amblin Group (Participant, Reliance, Entertainment One, Universal Pictures)
- CBS
- MGM

High-Profile Film Production Companies

In addition to the above, there are about sixteen high-profile film production companies that are either in-house branded arms (Fox 2000, Fox Animation, Fox Searchlight), studio-affiliated or independent financing and/or distribution shingles (such as Amazon Studios, Bold Films, IM Global, New Line, New Regency, Sierra Affinity). These firms have "deals"[1] with a select 150 reputable independent film production companies with great track records, many of which are star- or director-led. These could be some of your best, targeted points-of-entry prospects for your hit list.

High-Profile TV Production Companies

There are about forty in-house, affiliated or independent television production companies with development and production financing as well as distribution avenues:

• A+E Studios	• ABC Studios
• Amazon	• AMC Studios
• Apple	• BET Networks
• Bravo	• CBS TV Studios
• Comedy Central/ Viacom	• Critical Content
• Endemol Shine	• eOne

---

[1] Google *Variety*'s Facts on Pacts for a current list (or visit this book's constantly updated companion site, *HeatherHale.com/StorySelling*).

- FremantleMedia North America
- Gaumont
- HBO
- Imagine
- ITV Studios UK
- Lifetime
- MarVista Entertainment
- MTV/VH1
- OWN
- Platform One Media
- Sony Pictures TV
- Turner
- Universal Cable Prods.
- Warner Bros./Warner Horizon

- FX Prods.
- Global Road Entertainment
- Hulu
- ITV Studios America
- ITV America
- Lionsgate
- MGM
- Netflix
- Paramount TV
- Showtime
- Starz
- 20th Century Fox TV/Fox 21 TV Studios
- Universal TV

These forty have deals with just under one thousand production companies. These represent your best prospects.

The Top Baker's Dozen of International TV Buyers

As streaming networks have revolutionized the global TV landscape, huge mergers like 1) AT&T's acquisition of Time Warner, 2) Banijay Zodiak Nordic, and 3) Endemol Shine Group have consolidated it. Netflix currently has over 130 million subscribers in 190 countries. Amazon Prime has 100 million subscribers. While "only" at 20 million subscribers, Hulu has been breaking significant records with its live events and fine original programming.

There are a couple of ways of looking at today's major TV buyers. One would be by the number of production companies providing content to them; the other would be by their physical footprints in global territories. This eleven (or thirteen if you add Netflix and Amazon—Hulu's a part of NBCUniversal) dominate. To reiterate: You'd be looking at pitching to the production companies they have deals with, as shown below.

TV Production Company	# of Prod Cos/ Labels	TV Production Company	# of Territory Footprints
Endemol Shine Group	120	Fremantle	31
ITV Studios	60	Endemol Shine Group	30
Banijay	59	Warner Bros. Intl TV	17
Nice Entertainment Group	28	Banijay	16
Fremantle	25	Nice Entertainment Group	16
Red Arrow Ent	20	Sony Television Productions Int'l	13
All3Media	18	ITV Studios	9
Sony Television Productions Int'l	18	Red Arrow Ent	7
BBC Worldwide	17	BBC Worldwide	7
NBC Universal Int'l TV Production	5	All3Media	6
Warner Bros. Intl TV	3	NBC Universal Int'l TV Production	3

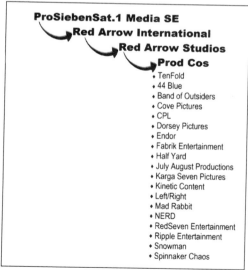

An example of one of Europe's leading media groups, Germany's second-largest privately-owned television company, Red Arrow, comprises 20 production companies in seven territories. They produce 485 shows amounting to 2,400 hours of TV a year.

Set Realistic Pitch Goals

Primary Goal: Elicit a script request (or book the
                       next meeting)
Secondary Goal: Network (build your relationships and
                       reputation, get intel)

With any entity you pitch, consider: *What do you want to get out of this meeting? Do you just want to sell the idea? Or actually go into business with them? Do you want to work on the show? And if so, in what capacity?*

Working together can evolve in lots of different ways. In television, it might involve an upfront fee, a fee per episode if it sells, a sliding scale based on how strong the project is or becomes based on how fully fleshed out it is or how involved you are in its further development.

Do you hold out hope to attach to direct your Ultra Low Budget feature? Or even if not the pilot, maybe you aspire to negotiate directing at least one episode per season? Maybe your rep just wants to ensure your WGA minimums for payment and credit.

Basic Pitch Architecture

While the journeys can feel frustratingly circuitous and actual execution vary wildly, the basic elements of pitching are fairly rudimentary.

Just as bearing walls carry the weight of a building, your pitch needs structure to support the weight of your idea and its verbal execution. As we've discussed, basic writing classes start with the inverted pyramid, imploring writers to start with the "hook" — the most important details first — then drill down to relevant contextual or background information. Police investigations, legal arguments, scholarly articles, technical writing, medical assessments, scientific research, executive summaries of business plans to even political speeches and debates all gather and funnel information in much the same way.

Sales and marketing missives follow a similar Bottom-Line Up-Front approach:

BLUF

1. Grab Attention
2. Build Anticipation
3. Call to Action

No matter who you're pitching to or what kind of material, you want to hook them with your headline idea — then take them somewhere. In your pitch, emulate the emotional roller-coaster experience you're promising for future viewers.

Pitch your heart out. You already poured it onto the page, right? This is the second course. Get your one sheet up on its feet. For each and every pitch, your challenge is to translate whatever it was about your idea that got so under your skin that you were compelled to dedicate months to years of your life to express the concept. No one can give you that passion. You should come preloaded with that. That should be why you're here: crazy enough to pursue this line of work. And remember: You're pitching to a person, not a company, culture or country.

Try not to use character names other than protagonist and maybe the antagonist. Refer to all the supporting characters via their relationship to your hero: "her boss," "his daughter," etc.

Who are we rooting for? What is their situation at the beginning of the script? How and where do we meet them in their everyday life? What new opportunity are they confronted with? Is there a visible goal that we will recognize as the story's finish line? Will it be clear if your protagonist won or lost? What inspired you to come up with the idea?

Are there any relevant antecedents worth mentioning to help establish the tone? And frame genre expectations?

While researching comps can be priceless to development, using them in an actual pitch can be *Risky Business. Know your audience.* Models you referenced for structure, theme or even casting inspiration may only be of interest to fellow writers. For the suits, don't mention their flops or even the labors of love of their predecessors. If you must, stick to genre, rating or tone touchstones that were box office or ratings hits that appeal to your same demographic.

If appropriate, capitalize on this rare one-on-one opportunity to get firsthand insights on what they're really looking for to ascertain future opportunities.

Don't Forget to Ask for the Order

"Coffee's for closers only."
Glengarry Glen Ross (1992)

CLOSE: *Would they like to read the script? Or do they have any questions?*

Questions Are Great Indicators

Great salespeople know that the closer you get to a deal, the more questions — and even objections — pop up. This is a good thing. Welcome them. Be prepared with clever, insightful answers. This is where all your pitch prep and practice will pay off. *What confused your friends when you pitched the first few times? Where were the slumps that bored practice listeners?* Hopefully, you've pruned all that out. Know what the tough questions will inevitably be in advance — and be prepared with kick-ass answers. Maybe even hold back a surprise twist, knowing that this will be an obvious question to ensure they participate — and you are locked and loaded to intrigue and delight.

If they say yes. . .? *Hallelujah!* and get the hell out of the room. *And get out of their line of sight before you do your jig!* A good salesman knows when to shut up. You cannot do any better than a "Yes." Hear that. Anything that comes out of your mouth after you've achieved your ultimate pitch goal will only risk their second-guessing their decision. Say "Thank you," shake their hands if it feels right — and *leave*. Be the first to leave the party.

If they have to pitch it further up the food chain (which inevitably they will), delicately offer that you'd be willing to come back and pitch it to whomever else needs to hear it. If they'll allow this, it takes the onus off them for their diluted copy of a copy performance and ensures nothing will be lost in translation. Not to mention: You get to begin to build a relationship with their boss, too.

If this pitch doesn't pan out, they might be able to save you a lot of time with your concept. *Maybe they have something similar in development? Or have the inside scoop of like projects already in production.* This can be priceless industry intel. When creatives pitch mismatched projects to me, I usually reveal who their most likely buyer candidates are to save all of us time.

Nervous?

Sure, you'll be nervous – especially if you're a writer rather than an actor or comedian. Before you pitch: practice, practice, practice. You cannot over-practice a pitch. Think of an actor who is so far off book they have the freedom and confidence to improvise. Be present in the moment. Engage with your scene partners.

You don't want your pitch coming across as memorized. Of course, it should be diligently structured and meticulously refined but you want to avoid referring to notes. Ideally, you are so well-prepared, it comes across as relaxed and casual — almost impromptu. Like you're telling a friend about this amazing film or TV show you saw, reveling in the drama, with the pure goal of getting them to be excited about seeing it, too.

Type up your pitch script. Handwrite it. Read it. Say it. Hear it. Record it. Muscle memory can help your mental memory. If you plot with 3" × 5" cards, create pitch-beat flash cards. Role play your pitch to a fellow screenwriting or producing buddy portraying your prospect. Record these practice pitch sessions for self-critique. In reviewing: *Can you integrate those answers to clarify your pitch? Or are they better left for the question and answer period?* Prepare excellent answers for anticipated questions you don't want to organically weave into the pitch. Watch the playback of your practice pitch. Like an athlete, study the playback. Painful as the feedback may be, it's also priceless.

Fix the pitch. Polish, polish, polish. Then practice some more. Make an MP4 of the audio recording and listen to it in your car, walk or jog to it. Rerecord your reading the flawless script and fall asleep to it. Envision your successful pitch. Journal the scene — including dialogue — of your successful pitch in the past tense as if it was already wildly successful. It's important. This could be life-changing.

Timing of Deliverables

Maybe your random elevator pitch at an event cocktail party resulted in business cards exchanged — and the emailed one sheet led to a script request. Awesome. That's one way. Some might even say textbook. But not. Really.

Other times (which might seem completely backwards, were it not so common): the pilot script and series bible are submitted by an agent and read by the decision-making team's front-runners. *Then* the writer is brought in — after the fact — to surreally verbally pitch from scratch what everyone already has sitting in front of them. Don't assume anyone's read anything. Initial notes could've been generated by a contracted reader. Be prepared to pitch from scratch.

If you're pitching cold or no one has seen any of your marketing materials, don't be too quick to hand them anything. You don't want to lessen your interpersonal engagement by offering up eye-contact distraction. Read the room. You might be better served to withhold your marketing materials and just absorb the insights gleaned during this precious one-on-one interaction. A PowerPoint *might* be a happy medium, if appropriate, as it allows you to share the images with the whole room as a group. It also allows you the opportunity to not only follow up with the PDF, but it gives you the chance to tweak your materials to integrate their revealed inclinations.

It's prudent to be a little precious with tape, too — especially for high-concept formats. Play it in the room but don't leave it for them to nitpick in your absence or worse: cherry-pick your efforts to refine their own overlapping projects.

Follow Up!

Ninety percent of salespeople don't follow up, but eighty percent of sales are made on the fifth to twelfth contact. If these oft-quoted figures are true, your marching numbers are pretty obvious. Look for good excuses to follow up. Delivering requested materials is the best reason.

Consider creating a Google Alert with their company, individual and project names to watch for opportunities to congratulate them for promotions, genuinely praise award nominations and wins, ratings successes. Try to attend their panel discussions, read blogs they're quoted in. You want to stay on their radar in a positive way — but don't be annoying. Keep your missives brief, constructive and on-point. You want the door to remain open for future pitches — and to subconsciously remind them of this project and your future availability for other projects.

Adapting to Different Scenarios and Environments

Your approach, pace and the architecture of each pitch will vary based on the venue and circumstances of each opportunity. The extent of noise and distraction can change the format of pitch. What will work on the market floor or at a crowded industry cocktail party might feel too rushed or audacious for an on-the-lot meeting or in an equity investor's private home. In an office, your presentation can be more relaxed, you can go deeper into things, add more video. On the market floor or in an elevator pitch (in line at Starbucks at a festival), you have to grab their attention immediately.

No matter the logistics, your verbal pitch and marketing materials should emulate the viewing experience in tone, pace and energy. Orient them immediately to your genre, format and subject matter. Your approach strategies will morph given the project, scenario, environment and goal.

Pitch Fests

Most pitch fests are loud, noisy hotbeds of chaotic, rushed desperation. But they can also be fun and entertaining. A great shot in the arm of inspiration. A great arbitrary deadline to catalyze completion for a creative. And great networking. A lot like speed dating (and equally as painful on both sides), the beauty to pitch fests is that everyone knows why everyone else is there and everyone is ready to get right down to business. A buffet of the good, the bad and the ugly to be sure. Some markets offer a higher quality matchmaking experience by vetting both ways, ensuring actual decision-making executives are hearing professionally prepared pitches. Make the most out of every opportunity.

Do Your Advance Due Diligence

Thoroughly review all the materials the event organizers provide. Usually this is the most up-to-date information available. It's what whomever is attending is looking for (which might be different than what other people at the same company might be looking for). These mandate matrices alone can sometimes be worth the price of admission.

Visit the catchers' websites, too. Find out as much as you can about who will be coming. On site, compare notes with peers who've already pitched to your targets to see if their intel might help you.

While ignoring a ballroom of simultaneous hawkers all around you, you have to get through your practiced spiel — a hyper-condensed speed version of an industry pitch meeting — in only a few minutes. Most are three to seven minutes, fifteen max. Greet them, build rapport as fast as possible — then get on with it. They know why you're both there — and that your time is oddly crunched.

Festivals, Conferences, and Markets

Some of your best networking can be with panelists and judges at meals or in between workshops or screenings. Attend as many of the event's breakfasts, lunches, cocktail parties as you can. Even if you're an introvert, you paid to be here (or got nominated), shore up your charm reserves and make the most of being away from your computer for a couple of days.

Pitching on a market floor can be crazy. Exhibitors and other attendees have meetings scheduled every fifteen to thirty minutes. Being on time is late. Get there early. And be prepared to be bumped. They're there to sell. Their prospects will trump your pitch. The more patient you have been, the more receptive they might be to hearing your pitch.

Don't schedule your meetings too close together — or too far apart geographically. Interactive, online market maps can be invaluable. Pay attention to hotel names, floors and suite numbers. Notice where you'll be for conferences and parties and try to schedule logistically.

Ask for people by name. Even if you don't know them, research online who has the most appropriate title you should be pitching to and get their name and try to book an appointment with them, specifically. If you can't suss this out from the online apps or printed guides, visit their booth or suite without introducing yourself. Pick up one sheets, catalogs, brochures, business cards. Study the company's culture. Call or email back to make an appointment with the right people who are there.[2]

There's a lot of noise — distractions all around. The more you can condense and communicate non-verbally, the better. One to two minutes, tops, for your actual pitch is ideal.

On-the-Lot Scheduled Pitches

The Holy Grail. Actual real buyers — hopefully with development money and access to distribution. One or more execs will have actually set aside time specifically for you, wanting to hear your specific pitch (that they might actually be interested in). Or perhaps they are looking — now or in the near future — to hire a writer like you.

---

[2] I wrote a whole book on this. Check out: *How to Work the Film & TV Markets: A Guide for Content Creators.*

Trust your material. You know it, especially if you wrote it. Relax. If you have practiced your pitch on your family, friends, writers' group and anyone who would listen — even strangers — you have a right to your earned confidence.

Now you've got a Hollywood eternity of fifteen to forty-five minutes to just squeeze in all of the following (in about this order): greetings, relevant and interesting intro, break the ice, build rapport, honestly acknowledge them for some of their work that you admire, don't rush but segue into the genesis or emotional inspiration for your project, slip in the title and genre to make sure they're oriented, knock that logline that you rewrote more than your script out of the park, and move gently into your well-rehearsed pitch making it seem like more of a conversation than a presentation. *Phew!* That's *"all"* you've got to do!

Hit a key milestone five minutes in and give them some mile markers: *"That's when we break to Act Two. . ."* Don't just list the events of your beat outline. They can read a beat sheet. They brought you in to entertain them with a story. As you weave through your key turning points, make them *feel* the twists and turns. Hopefully they're laughing if you're pitching a comedy or on the edge of their seats if it's a thriller. Emulate the viewing experience through your verbal storyselling just as you master on the page. Don't steamroll over them. *Engage their imagination.* Check in with them periodically. Ask questions. Show respect. *Is this the type of project they do or might be interested in?*

Don't Tell: Sell

sell, Sell, SELL!

Don't be so myopically focused on the artistic elements or even the structure that you lose sight of what everyone's in the room for: to discern how marketable what you're pitching is. *Can they make money off it?* It is show *business* after all.

Pitching Dos & Don'ts

DO. . .

- lead with an emotional hook.
- tell them what the show is *about*.
- stay top-note summary.
- come in with a complete vision for the entire series.
- focus on what the whole show is.
- be specific about this unique world.
- have a point of view.
- tell a story — in the broadest strokes — with a beginning, middle and end.
- be well-prepared and professional.
- answer their questions directly.
- be ready for whatever happens in the room.
- stay flexible.
- be passionate about your project. Genuine enthusiasm is contagious.

DON'T. . .

- be boring.
  - Don't just recite a verbal beat outline of the plot.
- confuse your prospect.
- be gimmicky.
- be delusional.
  Keep your budget, cast wish-list, price point/credit expectations realistic.
- get defensive.
  It's less important to be "right" than it is to pitch a show they will buy or develop.
- offend your prospects by arrogantly implying you can write/produce better.

- be coy: *"You'll have to read the script to find out how it ends!"*

  or: *"They'll have to wait and see the sequel!"*

Dos & Don'ts for Scripted Television Pitches

DO...

- focus on the characters.

  They are more important than the plot.

- provide the three-act structure of the first season or the whole series — anchored by your protagonist's arc.

DON'T...

- focus exclusively on the pilot plot.

  It's less about the pilot than where it goes from there.

Dos & Don'ts for Reality TV Pitches

DO...

- start with the reason behind the show.
  - *Why is this idea valid? What does it answer? A trend? An international need? A mood? A psychological atmosphere?*
- simply state the core idea of the format.
- compare your show to similar *successful* programming.
- reveal the storytelling mechanism.
- delve deeper into how it works.
- be versed in what your prospect, its siblings and competitors currently produce or distribute.
- highlight how your approach differs from their (or their competitors') content.
- point out your show's Unique Selling Proposition (USP).
- identify complementary programming possibilities.
- reveal how your program creates new opportunities in this space.

  Does your show create a whole new genre/format?
- be authentic.

- show how your program will connect audiences to real moments experienced by real people.
- pitch characters and character-driven dramatic conflict. Reality is about people — not issues. A show about a subject won't cut it.
- pitch unscripted characters who are engaging, root-worthy, inspiring, resilient and forward-thinking.
- be willing to adapt the pitch on the fly.

DON'T. . .

- pitch a show that is "better" than your prospect's existing show(s).
  "This is the new and improved [insert their show here]" might be true but that's not going to engender their comradery.
  Even if it's better than their competitors' shows, they are rarely looking for "the next" (*whatever*) – they are always looking for something fresh, innovative and original.
- be derisive of an entire genre, format or slate.
- come in "overly baked."
  If you hammer out seasons' worth of episodes, you leave little room for anyone else to dig in and discover the most sellable path.
- be earnest.
  Earnestness can come across as boring or old fashioned — the kiss of death in entertainment.
- pitch nasty, superficial, artificial, contrived conflict.
- pitch a reality TV show you have no idea how to make.
  - A screenwriter can absolutely pitch a scripted series (or feature) without the foggiest idea of what the budget might be or how to pull off the cinematics. This happens all the time and is a creative engine of the scripted business. But reality television producers and content

creators cannot come to the table without a vision-exe-
cution strategy.

SOCIAL EXPERIMENT

Social experiment shows are fairly easy to pitch verbally but
they are almost completely contingent on the producer's credibility in producing like programming.

FACTUAL PROGRAMMING

Factual programming can be among the easiest content to pitch
as it is so research-based. So literally matter of fact, you don't
want to risk it being dry or boring. Initial pitches are often best
served as top-note thumbnail sketches to ascertain a channel's interest. Listen and integrate their feedback. Come back
more fully fleshed out, customized specifically for their outlet's
demographics.

GAME SHOWS

It used to be far more common in a game show pitch meeting
for producers to have their prospects actually play the game.
Some even brought ballroom dancers "into the room." These
daring spectacles might be fun and engaging if they truly illustrate unique elements, but the stakes are equally high for it to
backfire, proving awkward for all parties and being off-putting
for your commissioner. Even hiring actors to portray prototype
contestants to run through a rehearsal demonstrating the game-
play mechanics will be far more appropriate and effective *after*
your financier/distributor has expressed initial interest.

Verbally describing quiz shows can be a disaster. Even the
most perfect trivia questions can be tedious when distilled as
an element of a live presentation. Consider creating a lower-
risk, limited-financial outlay, animated sizzle reel to pitch your
game show in a quick and visually interesting way.

PITCHING LARGER-THAN-LIFE REALITY TV PERSONALITIES

Audiences love larger-than-life personalities. But before viewers will click to watch a "Day in the Life of" unique families, businesses or avocations, producers must first convince financiers and distributors to gamble often millions on the potential marketability of these engaging characters in their intriguing milieus. Just like one-hour dramas and sitcoms, it all comes down to character. And their conflicts. Content creators must convince the Powers That Be that the everyday lives of this constellation of individuals will be filled with such conflict-rich, cinematic challenges that audiences will be compelled to watch episode after episode.

CELEBREALITY IS ALL ABOUT ACCESS

If you're basing the strength of your pitch on having a famous sports star, chef, high-profile host or other celebrity attached — *have them attached.* Don't misrepresent. Your connection not only needs to be solid, but it must be one that others can't easily replicate. While a relationship to talent can get you a deal, the talent has to actually be on board with the idea before you pitch. Don't take those relationships or that access for granted.

USE CAUTION BRINGING TALENT TO THE PITCH

Be careful having talent pitch for or with you. If they are partners or producers on the project, then — of course — that's appropriate. But an unofficial loose cannon may be "great in the room" but they might be more focused on selling themselves rather than your show (with or without *you* attached).

If the exec is intrigued by your show concept — but not the existing talent attachments — having that person sitting right there in the room inhibits a broader discussion of the concept, considering any other casting options.

A talent reel (even of just Skype audition clips) is often a more prudent strategy to express the full spectrum of possibilities and keep the discussion collaborative.

DETACHABLE ATTACHMENTS

Sometimes, it can be prudent to have *de*tachable "attachments" that allow you the freedom to offer up a short list of alternates or even just representative "types" as flexible options. Shows have certainly been successfully built around a given talent's personality and skills, but if your program is contingent upon that singular talent — and you encounter challenges with them, or the network doesn't connect with them — your entire venture could be derailed. If you originate a show based on a solid concept, you can cast a wide net to find alternate big characters that will help sell (or fill) that show concept.

FINAL THOUGHTS

Everyone's always looking for great original ideas, professionally executed by fresh voices.

Across all genres and formats: the pitch. The concept, the simpler it is, the easier it is to pitch, the more marketable to industry pros, the easier it will be to advertise to the viewing public.

But not every project is high concept.

If you have an amazing script and a terrific agent, you might be all set. An awesome one sheet and an excellent verbal pitch serves every project. You may never need anything else.

But not everyone has the luxury of a rep who works hard for them.

So much of creativity is DIY, fruition, the onus of the originator. The more informed you are, the better choices and decisions you can make. The more proficient you get at your craft and art, the more likely you'll be able to turn your avocation into your vocation.

Every component — from the title and shortest tagline to any images (moving or not) to the most involved spreadsheet — should be *crystal clear*, visually interesting and emotionally engaging.

The big commandments? Don't be boring. Don't confuse your reader, listener or viewer. Beyond that: Don't talk down to them or be obsequious. Be as concise as possible. Include only relevant information. Don't share a single word that might be a red flag. When in doubt, leave it out.

Macheting your way to the Powers That Be ain't for the fainthearted. These jungles are full of bewildering, untrodden paths. Yet, everyday, there's a new inspiring story of how someone else uniquely broke in to the biz or (finally) enjoyed a triumphant success.

There are no definitive "right" or "wrong" ways.

There's just luck.

And timing.

But you can create your own opportunities.

And prepare for any you might be able to generate.

Produce your own career.

If a terrific script was flung from an airplane — Hollywood would find it. Your calling dictates that you get the very best version of your brilliant project on the right radars, in ways that the right people will respond to your vision.

Keep creating.

Keep connecting.

Keep finding meaning.

The world needs your stories.

ABOUT THE AUTHOR

Heather Hale is a film and television producer, director, screenwriter, teacher
and consultant. She directed, produced
and co-wrote the million-dollar indie
thriller *Absolute Killers* (2011) which
starred Meatloaf, Edward Furlong,
and Ed Asner and was marketed at Le
Marché du Film and the American Film
Market. She wrote the 5.5 million-dollar
Lifetime Original Movie *The Courage to*

Love that starred Vanessa Williams, Stacey Keach, Gil Bellows,
and Diahann Carrol and has over 60 hours of produced reality
credits which have won Emmys, Ace, and Telly awards. Her
How to Work the Film & TV Markets: A Guide for Content Cre-
ators was published by Focal Press/Routledge in 2017. She was
the Director of Programming for the National Association of
Television Program Executives, and was the Independent Film
and Television Alliance's Industry Liaison for the 2013 American Film Market (AFM) and had a four-year development deal
with NBCUniversal (through IFTA).

Helpful *StorySelling* resources are shared on her site at:
https://heatherhale.com/storyselling. If you'd like Ms. Hale to
speak at your event or to hire her as a consultant, contact her
at Heather@HeatherHale.com.

SAVE THE CAT! ®
THE LAST BOOK ON SCREENWRITING YOU'LL EVER NEED!

BLAKE SNYDER

BEST SELLER

He's made millions of dollars selling screenplays to Hollywood and now screenwriter Blake Snyder tells all. "Save the Cat!®" is just one of Snyder's many ironclad rules for making your ideas more marketable and your script more satisfying — and saleable, including:

· The four elements of every winning logline.
· The seven immutable laws of screenplay physics.
· The 10 genres and why they're important to your movie.
· Why your Hero must serve your idea.
· Mastering the Beats.
· Mastering the Board to create the Perfect Beast.
· How to get back on track with ironclad and proven rules for script repair.

This ultimate insider's guide reveals the secrets that none dare admit, told by a show biz veteran who's proven that you can sell your script if you can save the cat.

"Imagine what would happen in a town where more writers approached screenwriting the way Blake suggests? My weekend read would dramatically improve, both in sellable/producible content and in discovering new writers who understand the craft of storytelling and can be hired on assignment for ideas we already have in house."
   —From the Foreword by Sheila Hanahan Taylor, Vice President, Development at Zide/Perry
      Entertainment, whose films include *American Pie, Cats and Dogs, Final Destination*

"One of the most comprehensive and insightful how-to's out there. Save the Cat!® is a must-read for both the novice and the professional screenwriter."
   —Todd Black, Producer, *The Pursuit of Happyness, The Weather Man, S.W.A.T, Alex and
      Emma, Antwone Fisher*

"Want to know how to be a successful writer in Hollywood? The answers are here. Blake Snyder has written an insider's book that's informative — and funny, too."
   —David Hoberman, Producer, *The Shaggy Dog (2005), Raising Helen, Walking Tall, Bringing
      Down the House, Monk (TV)*

BLAKE SNYDER, besides selling million-dollar scripts to both Disney and Spielberg, was one of Hollywood's most successful spec screenwriters. Blake's vision continues on *www.blakesnyder.com.*

$21.95 · 216 PAGES · ORDER NUMBER 34RLS · ISBN: 9781932907001

FILM DIRECTING: SHOT BY SHOT
VISUALIZING FROM CONCEPT TO SCREEN

25TH ANNIVERSARY EDITION

STEVEN D. KATZ

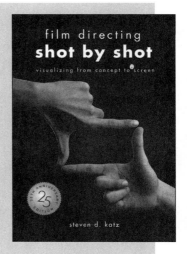

Shot by Shot is the world's go-to directing book, now newly updated for a special 25th Anniversary edition! The first edition sold over 250,000 copies, making it one of the bestselling books on film directing of all time. Aspiring directors, cinematographers, editors, and producers, many of whom are now working professionals, learned the craft of visual storytelling from *Shot by Shot*, the most complete source for preplanning the look of a movie.

The book contains over 800 photos and illustrations, and is by far the most comprehensive look at shot design in print, containing storyboards from movies such as *Citizen Kane*, *Blade Runner*, *Deadpool*, and *Moonrise Kingdom*. Also introduced is the concept of A, I, and L patterns as a way to simplify the hundreds of staging choices facing a director in every scene.

Shot by Shot uniquely blends story analysis with compositional strategies, citing examples then illustrated with the storyboards used for the actual films. Throughout the book, various visual approaches to short scenes are shown, exposing the directing processes of our most celebrated auteurs — including a meticulous, lavishly illustrated analysis of Steven Spielberg's scene design for *Empire of the Sun*.

Overall, the book has new storyboards and concept art, rewritten text for several chapters to address the needs of the YouTube generation of filmmakers, and an enhanced, expanded list of filmmaking resources.

· New introduction
· New storyboards: *Moonrise Kingdom*, *Deadpool*
· Six rewritten chapters detailing new trends and new digital production tools
· New section: Short Cuts
· Visual update: Dozens of illustrations are now shaded to maximize readability
· New bibliography
· New list of online resources

STEVEN D. KATZ is an award-winning writer, producer, and director. His work has appeared on *Saturday Night Live* and in many cable and theatrically released films, such as *Clear and Present Danger*, for which he completed the first full digital previsualization of a motion picture. He has taught workshops at the American Film Institute, Sundance Film Festival, Parsons School of Design, Danish Film Institute, School for Visual Arts (in New York), and Shanghai University, among many others.

$31.95 · 400 PAGES · ISBN 9781615932979

DIRECTING ACTORS
CREATING MEMORABLE PERFORMANCES
FOR FILM AND TELEVISION

JUDITH WESTON

BEST SELLER
OVER 45,000 COPIES SOLD!

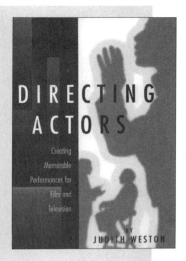

Directing film or television is a high-stakes occupation. It captures your full attention at every moment, calling on you to commit every resource and stretch yourself to the limit. It's the white-water rafting of entertainment jobs. But for many directors, the excitement they feel about a new project tightens into anxiety when it comes to working with actors.

This book provides a method for establishing creative, collaborative relationships with actors, getting the most out of rehearsals, troubleshooting poor performances, giving briefer directions, and much more. It addresses what actors want from a director, what directors do wrong, and constructively analyzes the director-actor relationship.

"Judith Weston is an extraordinarily gifted teacher."
> — David Chase, Emmy® Award-Winning Writer,
> Director, and Producer *The Sopranos,*
> *Northern Exposure, I'll Fly Away*

"I believe that working with Judith's ideas and principles has been the most useful time I've spent preparing for my work. I think that if Judith's book were mandatory reading for all directors, the quality of the director-actor process would be transformed, and better drama would result."
> — John Patterson, Director
> *Six Feet Under, CSI: Crime Scene Investigation,*
> *The Practice, Law and Order*

"I know a great teacher when I find one! Everything in this book is brilliant and original and true."
> — Polly Platt, Producer, *Bottle Rocket*
> Executive Producer, *Broadcast News, The War of the Roses*

JUDITH WESTON was a professional actor for 20 years and has taught Acting for Directors for over a decade.

$29.95 · 314 PAGES · ORDER NUMBER 4RLS · ISBN: 0941188248

SAVE THE CAT! GOES TO THE MOVIES

THE SCREENWRITER'S GUIDE TO EVERY STORY EVER TOLD

BLAKE SNYDER

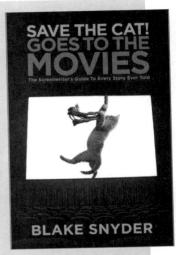

In the long-awaited sequel to his surprise bestseller, *Save the Cat!*, author and screenwriter Blake Snyder returns to form in a fast-paced follow-up that proves why his is the most talked-about approach to screenwriting in years. In the perfect companion piece to his first book, Snyder delivers even more insider's information gleaned from a 20-year track record as "one of Hollywood's most successful spec screenwriters," giving you the clues to write *your* movie.

Designed for screenwriters, novelists, and movie fans, this book gives readers the key breakdowns of the 50 most instructional movies from the past 30 years. From *M*A*S*H* to *Crash*, from *Alien* to *Saw*, from *10* to *Eternal Sunshine of the Spotless Mind*, Snyder reveals how screenwriters who came before you tackled the same challenges you are facing with the film you want to write — or the one you are currently working on.

Writing a "rom-com"? Check out the "Buddy Love" chapter for a "beat for beat" dissection of *When Harry Met Sally...* plus references to 10 other great romantic comedies that will make your story sing.

Want to execute a great mystery? Go to the "Whydunit" section and learn about the "dark turn" that's essential to the heroes of *All the President's Men*, *Blade Runner*, *Fargo* and hip noir *Brick* — and see why ALL good stories, whether a Hollywood blockbuster or a Sundance award winner, follow the same rules of structure outlined in Snyder's breakthrough method.

If you want to sell your script and create a movie that pleases most audiences most of the time, the odds increase if you reference Snyder's checklists and see what makes 50 films tick. After all, both executives and audiences respond to the same elements good writers seek to master. They want to know the type of story they signed on for, and whether it's structured in a way that satisfies everyone. It's what they're looking for. And now, it's what you can deliver.

BLAKE SNYDER, besides selling million-dollar scripts to both Disney and Spielberg, is still "one of Hollywood's most successful spec screenwriters," having made another spec sale in 2006. An in-demand scriptcoach and seminar and workshop leader, Snyder provides information for writers through his website, *www.blakesnyder.com*.

$22.95 · 270 PAGES · ORDER NUMBER 75RLS · ISBN: 1932907351

THE MYTH OF MWP

In a dark time, a light bringer came along, leading the curious and the frustrated to clarity and empowerment. It took the well-guarded secrets out of the hands of the few and made them available to all. It spread a spirit of openness and creative freedom, and built a storehouse of knowledge dedicated to the betterment of the arts.

The essence of the Michael Wiese Productions (MWP) is empowering people who have the burning desire to express themselves creatively. We help them realize their dreams by putting the tools in their hands. We demystify the sometimes secretive worlds of screenwriting, directing, acting, producing, film financing, and other media crafts.

By doing so, we hope to bring forth a realization of 'conscious media' which we define as being positively charged, emphasizing hope and affirming positive values like trust, cooperation, self-empowerment, freedom, and love. Grounded in the deep roots of myth, it aims to be healing both for those who make the art and those who encounter it. It hopes to be transformative for people, opening doors to new possibilities and pulling back veils to reveal hidden worlds.

MWP has built a storehouse of knowledge unequaled in the world, for no other publisher has so many titles on the media arts. Please visit www.mwp.com where you will find many free resources and a 25% discount on our books. Sign up and become part of the wider creative community!

Onward and upward,

Michael Wiese
Publisher/Filmmaker